DEVON AND CORNWALL RECORD SOCIETY
New Series, Vol. 21

T0385883

DEVON AND CORNWALL RECORD SOCIETY

New Series, Vol. 21

A Calendar of
EARLY CHANCERY PROCEEDINGS
relating to
WEST COUNTRY SHIPPING
1388–1493

Edited with an Introduction by

DOROTHY M. GARDINER

Printed for the Society by
THE DEVONSHIRE PRESS LTD.
TORQUAY

1976

The transcripts and translations of Crown-copyright
records in this edition appear by permission of the
Controller of H.M. Stationery Office and the Keeper
of the Public Records.

CONTENTS

REFERENCES AND ABBREVIATIONS

MANUSCRIPT (PUBLIC RECORD OFFICE)

S.C.8   Ancient Petitions

PRINTED

Avery, M. E., 1969   Proceedings in the court of chancery.
                               Bulletin of the Institute of Historical Research,
                               Vol. XLII No. 106

Baildon, W. P. (ed.), 1896   *Select cases in chancery A.D. 1364–1471*
                               (Selden Society Publications No. X)

Baldwin, J. F., 1913   *The king's council in England during the middle
                               ages*

CCR   *Calendar of Close Rolls 1227–1509*

CPR   *Calendar of Patent Rolls 1232–1566*

Foed.   *Foedera*, Rymer, T. (ed.), 1704, Vols. XI, XII

Gairdner, J., 1910   *The Paston Letters*, Vol. I

Kingsford, C. L., 1925   *Prejudice and promise in the 15th century England*

Marsden, R. G. (ed.), 1892   *Select pleas in the court of admiralty*
                               (Selden Society Publications No. 6)

Marsden, R. G., 1894   *Law and custom of the sea* (Navy Record Society)

Maxwell-Lyte, H. C., 1901   *List of Early Chancery Proceedings* Vol. I
                               (Lists and Indexes XII)

Maxwell-Lyte, H. C., 1926   *Historical notes on the use of the great seal of
                               England* (H.M. Stationery Office)

Nicolas, N. H., 1847   *History of the Royal Navy*, Vol. II

Rot. Parl.   *Rotuli Parliamentorum*, Vols. IV, V

Twiss, T. (ed.), 1874   *The Black Book of the Admiralty* (Rolls Series)
                               Vol. III

Vale, M. G. A., 1970   *English Gascony 1399–1453*

Veale, E. W. W. (ed.),   *Great Red Book of Bristol* Text parts I and II
   1933, 1938   (Bristol Record Society Publications Vols.
                               IV, VIII)

Watkin, R. H., 1935   *Dartmouth I Pre-reformation* (Devonshire As-
                               sociation: parochial histories 5)

INTRODUCTION

DESCRIPTION OF THE DOCUMENTS

The documents classified as Early Chancery Proceedings at the Public Record Office relate to the judicial work of the chancery during the period from the middle of the reign of Richard II until the end of that of Philip and Mary, i.e. about 1380 to 1558. They consist of plaintiffs' petitions and, after the first half of the fifteenth century—before which they were not usually put into writing—some of the defendants' answers and of those formal ' replications', 'rejoinders ' etc. which the procedure of the court might require from both parties. They include also decrees and orders of the court and some records of the proceedings which arose from them. They are not a class which has come down to us as it stands among the records of the chancery, but one that has been put together from four overlapping sources.[1] They are documents which were very carelessly kept in early times and as a result of this, and a highly complicated method of filing at a later date, many have been lost.[2]

A printed index (*Lists and Indexes Nos. XII and XVI, Early Chancery Proceedings Nos. I and II*) gives the names of the parties, a brief indication of the cause of each complaint and the place of its origin. The proceedings involving the seafaring activities of men of Devon and Cornwall and their ships can therefore be easily extracted. The majority of them are well written on strips of parchment of varying shapes and sizes—the most usual being long and narrow with the writing running horizontally along the strip. The state of their preservation varies also, some are in excellent condition—as easy to read as the day when they were written— others are creased and defaced and often, in spite of skilful repair, very difficult to decipher. Some are mutilated and parts of the script may be missing. There are 139 of them separately listed in the index, each of which, as a general rule, relates to a different complaint, but two or more of the documents belong to the same incident in 17 cases so that the total number of separate proceedings is 97. They are all found between the beginning of the series and 1493. Memoranda and notes of action taken by the court are entered at the foot of the document, or endorsed in a few cases, and six of them, dated in the second half of the fifteenth century, include records of the answers, replications and rejoinders of the parties; with these exceptions, the calendar consists of petitions (or bills as they came to be called) seeking the assistance of the chancellor in the redress of grievances and reparation for loss or injury inflicted by one individual or group of individuals on another.[3]

---

[1] Maxwell-Lyte 1901 Preface.
[2] Baldwin 1913, p. 263.
[3] One only (No. 8) sought a remedy for loss caused by the crown, i.e. arrest of a barge, without payment, for the king's service.

FORM AND LANGUAGE OF THE PETITIONS

The first 23 petitions, i.e. from 1388 to about 1430, are all in French; from number 24 to 39 (about 1437) English and French alternate after which, with one or two exceptions, English is the language used. The occasional memoranda and notes of action taken by the court are usually in Latin.

Each petition is headed with an address to the chancellor currently in office—nearly always a bishop—and is composed of a complaint followed by a request for action of some kind. The complaints, which begin with the petitioners' names and give their home towns and sometimes their occupations, are expressed very freely and the requests vary to suit the nature of the grievances, but both sections are introduced by forms of words so nearly similar in each document that they have not been set out in the calendar. The words of each address are also the same in sentiment and style and have been omitted, but they like the other introductory words vary a little in effusiveness. For example, the chancellor might be *tres reverent piere en dieu et mon tresgracious seigneur l'evesque de . . . chaunceller dengleterre* which in English became *the reverent fader in god and my gracious lord the bishop of . . . chanceler of Englond*; or *tres honore et tres reverent piere en dieu levesque de . . .*, the English equivalents being *my right good lord Thomas, Archbishop . . ., the most worshipfull fader yn God the Archbishop . . .* or bishop, or some similar variation in more or less extravagant terms.[1] They do not often include the bishop's name and the date of the actual presentation of the document in court does not appear, nevertheless the practice of addressing the chancellor by his title, be it his diocese or—when occasionally a layman held the office— some other designation, allows the *Index of the Early Chancery Proceedings* to be compiled in roughly chronological order: roughly only, because, although a list of chancellors with their dates is included in the volume,[2] the incumbent of the same bishopric not infrequently held office as chancellor at different times and often for a number of years; there are, moreover, some petitions addressed only to *the chancellor of England*. As with the addresses, there were elaborations on the form of words introducing the complaints. These increased as the fifteenth century progressed. *Supplie humblement* (or *tres humblement*) *J. E. of W. merchant, qe comme . . .* is typical of the earliest documents calendared and, translated into English as: *besecheth mekely* (or *fulle mekely*) *T.S. of D. that how . . .* continues in use throughout the period covered. The earliest and most often used variation was *supplie humblement votre pover oratour* (*J.Q. marchant natif et demourant etc. in Lisbon*, e.g. 22, 32 below): or in an earlier version *supplie humblement votre treshumble servitour* (17) in the English versions ' bedeman '[3] is sometimes found, e.g. *right mekely besekes unto your gracious lordship your power bedman, R.B. merchant that where etc . . .* or more simply: *besecth lowly your pore bedeman W.N. of etc. . . .* (58) The word ' oretour ' was however most frequently used—in English as in the French documents

---

[1] E.g. The petition of the attorney of merchants of Rouen, c. 1432, is headed: *tres reverend pere en dieu tres hault tres excellerent et tres puissant prellat monsieur levesque de bath.*

[2] Maxwell-Lyte , *op. cit.*, p. vii.

[3] i.e. a petitioner=your humble servant.

—as *beseching mekely and lowly your oratour R.C.* etc. (52) or similar phrases emphasizing the humble state of the petitioner. In some cases from the middle of the century on, *showeth* was substituted for *besecheth*, e.g. *mekely showeth unto you . . .* (61, 73) or occasionally: *sheweth and lamentably complaineth unto your good lordship.* . . . One fourteenth century complaint began rather obscurely: *monstre petousement ensoy complaignant votre povere desease subjet R.S. de D. que come etc . . .* (2), words which can only be intended to stress the grievous circumstances which had brought the petitioner into court—injuries caused by physical assault having been part of them.

The request which brought each petition to a close began with a brief entreaty which varied only slightly, i.e. *qe plese a votre tresgracious seigneur . . .* (1, 3) being in English: *like (or please) hit to youre worshipful and gracious lordship . . .* (42, 43) or *may it please youre most gracious lordship to graunt.,* etc. There is always a final invocation of God, and nearly always of *the way (or work) of charity.* In the last ten petitions, presented between 1475 and 1493, the requests are made in terms so similar to each other that they virtually amount to a formula: writs are applied for by their Latin names, not, as had been usual at the beginning of the century, in some such words as: *grauntier brief pour faire venir le dit (defendant) devant vous,* etc. . . . (12) *graunt a writte under a sufficient peyne direct to (the defendant) to appere etc.* . . . (36) Decisions are always required to be in accordance with *right (or reason) and good conscience,* whereas in earlier documents these words are often omitted or introduced in much less stereotyped ways. In the later complaints, particulars of incidents and descriptions of goods seized or injuries caused are given with much more precision and the documents are altogether more professional in style than those written earlier, many of which suggest that they were taken down exactly as dictated by the petitioners. But from first to last, petitions which do not conform to the usual pattern can be found. As far as possible the style of the original has been followed in translation, in order to indicate these variations in form.

PETITIONS IN THE CHANCERY

Petitions of this kind had, of course, long been the accepted means of seeking the king's justice. From the time of the Conquest, suitors had exercised the right to come to the king in his council when the local courts and customary laws proved inadequate and set out their grievances and seek for remedy.

Originally made orally, their complaints were at an early stage being received by the chancellor—secretary to the king and keeper of the great seal—and put into writing by clerks of the chancery. They were addressed as a rule to the king or the king and council, and it was one of the duties of councillors to hear the complaints and decide on remedies for those plaintiffs who had been wronged.[1] The petitions were returned to the chancery where writs and mandates to local officials and others, ordering them to bring the parties into court and to take such action or execute such judgements as had been awarded, were issued under the great seal

[1] Baldwin, *op. cit.,* p. 65.

and those which for any reason it was wished to put on record were entered on the patent or close rolls. During the twelfth and thirteenth centuries, as the business of the king's court increased, measures were taken to deal more efficiently with the complaints of private suitors: itinerant justices were appointed and regular circuits were introduced; justices were also commissioned to remain at Westminster permanently to hear the complaints of the people and to become later the court known as the common bench. Meanwhile justices and members of the council who formed the court *coram rege*, forerunner of the king's bench, continued to follow the king on his travels about the country. Both the common bench and, more slowly, the court *coram rege* developed into separate branches of the king's court, distinct from the council, administering the common law according to clearly defined and strictly observed rules. The judges derived their powers not from membership of the council, but from their commissions which set the limits of their authority. No case could be brought before them without a writ from chancery which set out exactly the cause of the required legal action. This had the effect eventually, in the course of the development of the business of their courts, of restricting the complaints that they could try to those for which a writ had been devised; by the end of the fourteenth century it had come about that unless the facts of a plaintiff's grievance could be made to fit the form of one of the recognized writs he would find himself without a remedy at common law. Proceedings by petition to the king's council were however still open to him, but if it was considered that his case could be dealt with by what had become the normal procedure, then it was to the common law courts that he must go.[1]

There were, of course, reasons other than the rigidity of their rules which could prevent the common law courts from providing justice and petitions continued to be received in large numbers.[2] All the administrative work continued to be the responsibility of the chancellor, whose office was by this time established at Westminster,[3] and certain kinds of cases were being referred to him for consideration and decision. By the beginning of Richard II's reign petitioners were frequently addressing their petitions to the chancellor himself and entreating him personally for remedy. This was a natural consequence of the influential position which he had long held in the judicial proceedings of the council, and, no doubt, of the stormy relationships between the kings and the lords of the council which characterized the period. Petitions continued to be addressed to the king and council and heard by them, but the practice of seeking the chancellor's aid directly increased rapidly during the following century, and his exclusive jurisdiction over certain kinds of action came to be recognized.[4] The west country proceedings calendared below came from this early and incomplete stage in the development of an independent court of chancery.

[1] *Ibid.*, pp. 47 ff and 236 ff. Cp. 70c below.
[2] Many thousands of them are preserved at the Public Record Office in the class Ancient Petitions (S.C.8). They are indexed under the names of the petitioners only so that their contents cannot be identified unless corroborative documents can be found.
[3] Maxwell-Lyte 1926, p. 17.
[4] Baldwin, *op. cit.*, p. 252. Avery, 1969, pp. 130–31.

CONTENT OF THE PETITIONS AND THEIR BACKGROUND

The petitions are not concerned with questions of law or procedure or any principles governing the right and conscience to which they constantly appeal. Their object is solely to set out, in a way as favourable as possible to the case of each petitioner—and omitting anything likely to help his adversary—the circumstances which had led to an alleged wrong, and to ask for the chancellor's help in obtaining a remedy. Since those calendared here are only a small number of the total in the class of Early Chancery Proceedings, which is itself incomplete, great caution must be used in founding any general theories on them without supporting evidence; moreover maritime cases, like any others, were brought before the king and council or the chancellor when redress was not available elsewhere, so that the wrongs of which they complain tend to have unusual features and are not a typical sample of litigation arising out of the day to day transactions of merchants and seamen. Nevertheless, taken one with another and related as they often can be with the enrolled orders and commissions issued by the court, they indicate a little of what actually happened both in the chancery and in the ports, and provide some useful illustrations of the way the laws and customs of the sea and the measures taken by the government to regulate maritime activities in a time of active warfare were carried out.

The responsibility for enforcing shipping regulations lay, of course, in the first instance with the officials—water bailiffs, collectors of customs and others—appointed by the crown in the seaports and with the mayors and bailiffs and other local officials who had jurisdiction over maritime and all other suits in their courts. It will be seen that many of the petitioners had recourse to the chancellor after proceedings in a mayor's court had proved ineffective, or with allegations of malpractices of officials who could not be called to account without the chancellor's aid since the privileges of their offices exempted them from obeying the ordinary common law writs (e.g. 1, 2, 4, 31, 43, etc.).

Offences committed in ships when at sea were dealt with in the court of the admiralty. The first commission to give an admiral power to hear plaints and do justice in maritime causes was issued in 1360; it was also the first to give the command of the ships of both the northern and western ports to one man instead of to two which had been the previous practice, and was done again frequently until early in the fifteenth century. From then on the office of admiral of England was usually given to a nobleman of high rank who remained in general command although captains or admirals might be appointed to take charge of fleets which were assembled for particular expeditions. From 1360 also the admirals' commissions had authorized them to appoint deputies capable of carrying out all their duties when they were otherwise occupied,[1] and it was these deputies or lieutenants who carried out the admiralty business, including holding the courts. Their activities are illustrated in petitions throughout the century and reflect to some extent the development which was taking place in the administration of the court.

Complaints, made in parliament, that the admirals had been exceeding

[1] Marsden, 1892, p. xlii. Nicolas, 1847, p. 127.

the limits of their jurisdiction resulted in statutes being passed in 1390 and 1392 which defined their powers and restricted their authority to offences committed at sea with no extension to anything done in the body of the counties.[1] The grievances from west country ports presented in chancery at about this time were not, however, of admiralty encroachment but of the difficulty in getting execution of the orders of the court, although it is possible that this sometimes had its origin in opposition to the exercise of the admiral's jurisdiction within the boundaries of the towns concerned. Between 1391 and 1394, a sergeant-at-arms who had been commissioned by the admiral, was accused of neglecting to carry out a judgement of the court against John Sampson of Plymouth (3). William Benteley, said to have been lieutenant of the king's admiral in 1397 (6), described some years later the repeated obstruction he had encountered before and after he had succeeded in carrying out the king's order as well as a commission from the admiral of England to arrest the same John Sampson, which he had done in Moretonhampstead. Sampson had been accused ' before the king ' of treasons and felonies committed at sea. His case had presumably been referred to the admiral to whom Benteley eventually brought him (12). A few years later there was a vice-marshal of the ' admiralty court in Devonshire ' who was authorized by warrant of the court to arrest a certain Breton, and complained of forcible resistance to the arrest and maltreatment afterwards (13, cp. 23). This was when Sir Thomas Beaufort was both admiral of England and chancellor, and at a time when the business of the court had been increasing,[2] and the appointment of additional personnel may well have been required. A Portuguese merchant who had been arrested in Dartmouth, *circ.* 1430, named three men as deputies of the admiral there (22) and, although this was probably incorrect, it seems that a deputy or lieutenant was responsible for a specific section of the coast and held courts when and where they were required within it.[3] Only one petitioner complained of being brought into the admiralty court for offences which had been done within the body of the county and that one not until after 1475, by which time there was an appointed judge of the admiralty, and Horton or Orton Key in Southwark had become the accustomed place for holding the court (87).

The majority of the proceedings in the calendar resulted from the taking at sea of ships and their cargoes and were the outcome of the state of warfare which—though interrupted by intervals of truce—was the usual relationship between England and France from 1337 until 1475. All the countries along the north-west coast of Europe were involved from time to time as allies or enemies of one side or the other, and the provision of ships both for military and other expeditions and to protect the coast and trading ships from enemy raiders was part of the ordinary occupation of ship-owners and seamen of all coasts, particularly those along the English Channel. Ships from elsewhere were requisitioned as well as theirs when fleets were required for the king's service beyond the

---

[1] Marsden, *op. cit.*, pp. l, 17.
[2] *Ibid.*, p. lii.
[3] Courts were held at Lostwithiel and Bridgewater, *Ibid.*, pp. 3, 17.

sea, but the safeguard of their own coasts and trade from the French and
marauding Normans and Bretons at times when the war was active was
left largely to the inhabitants of the ports. Sea-roving—i.e. scouring the
sea for enemy vessels—was a necessary employment for their ships which
had to be paid for by the taking of booty.

All kinds of ships were arrayed for war at the expense of their owners
assisted by victuallers from the surrounding neighbourhood and sent out
singly or in twos and threes or larger groups. A truce with France was
operative at the time of Henry IV's accession, but hostilities with Scotland
caused him to call upon the inhabitants of the southern and western ports
to follow the example of the Cinque Ports and men of the north to array
and arm vessels to support him in the war; without pay it seems, but with
permission to keep for themselves and the captors all that their ships
captured.[1] The Bretons were breaking the truce at sea, the French were
giving assistance to Welsh and Scottish rebels .and the government were
encouraging shipowners to arm their ships and retaliate.[2] In such
conditions failure to distinguish between the vessels and cargoes of
friends and those of the enemy was inevitable. Any ship or cargo belonging
to an enemy country or one that was disregarding a truce was, of course,
lawful prize, but an enemy ship with a cargo owned by merchants of a
kingdom covered by a recently made treaty of friendship or temporary
truce, or the discovery of enemy owned goods among the cargo of a
friend's ship could give rise to endless disputes.

Maritime laws and customs internationally accepted at the end of the
fourteenth century laid down the rules governing the capture of ships
and cargoes: according to these the master of an English ship coming
upon an enemy vessel and finding goods from an allied country might
agree with the owner of such cargo or his representative to ransom the
ship; if he would not—or more probably could not—do so, the captor
was entitled to take the ship and contents to his home port, where he
must deliver the cargo to its owners who, for their part, must pay him
the freight for the completed journey. When it was the ship which
belonged to the friend and the cargo to the enemy, it was lawful for the
captor to compel its master and crew to bring it to a place of safety where
they must surrender the enemy goods, but the ship and any other goods
must be released and the captor must pay the freight due on the surrendered goods.[3] Refusal to submit to the search by the captor ship
which these rules required rendered any vessel liable to be treated as
enemy and therefore lawful prize. The 'force and arms' referred to in
many of the petitions was a formal term, and in most cases probably
meant only that the captor ship was better arrayed for war than its
victim and would have been able to overpower it if opposed. The crew
of a ship who attacked and carried off a vessel or goods of an allied
country or of their own people without reason—i.e. who committed a
plainly piratical act—were, if caught, treated as criminals, and might be
sent to the king's bench (cp. 71j); if such an incident took place at sea,

---

[1] *CCR 1399–1402*, p. 168, *CPR 1399–1402*, p. 349. The king received one third of
prizes taken by ships in his pay. Cp. No. 7.

[2] *CPR 1401–5*, p. 298.

[3] Twiss 1874 pp. 539 *ff.*

however, it would be a case for the admiralty court, which would have
jurisdiction also over allegations that English subjects had failed, when
seizing enemy ships at sea, to observe the maritime laws governing the
rights of allies, but little evidence for this survives since regular admiralty
court records do not begin until the sixteenth century.[1]

The west country complaints concerning captures which were brought
into chancery were so varied and complicated that classification is
impossible, but certain features are implicit in most of them: a captured
ship—enemy or allied—had been brought into an English harbour or
port by a ship or ships working on their own to be disposed of, within the
body of the country, for the benefit of the captors and any others who were
entitled by maritime law to a share. A claim by the master of the prize
or by the owners of all or part of its cargo that the vessel or goods were
not enemy property had been rejected by the captors, and either because
the master and owners had complained to the local authorities seeking
that the disputed property should be arrested or for some other reason,
it had been put into safe custody until a pronouncement had been made
on their claim. The statute of 1353 referred to by several of the petitioners
(e.g. 65, 72b), gave the owners of unlawfully captured cargo the right to
recover it on giving proof of their ownership by their marks or by documents or by other reliable merchants without any other suit at common
law, but, as cases in the calendar illustrate, recovery of the goods did not
always follow. It might have been prevented by the deliberate removal
of the cargo beyond the jurisdiction of the port officials; or restitution
might have been refused because the offered proofs were considered to
be inadequate, or because circumstances justifying the capture had been
alleged. For one reason or another the aggrieved party had not received
the satisfaction to which he claimed to be entitled by the maritime laws,
and found himself without redress unless he sought the aid of the chancellor
or, much more frequently, the king and council.

Petitions were received by the latter in considerable numbers [2] during
the early part of the fifteenth century when relationships between England
and the countries across the channel were very precarious. Short term
extensions of the treaty with France were made as well as truces with
Brittany and other states. In 1414, after Henry V had made a temporary
truce with France, a statute was passed which enacted that truce breaking
and the disregard of safe conducts and the hiding and maintaining of
those who had offended should be considered high treason.[3] It provided
for conservators of the truce to be appointed in all ports by the crown and
under the admiral to inquire into breaches of the truce and safe conducts
and to punish the guilty; they had also to cause all masters of vessels and
their owners, if accompanying them, to take oath before leaving port that
they would do nothing against the truce or the king's safe conducts. The
conservators were to be informed of all things captured from the king's
enemies, which must be brought into port and shown to them before
being unloaded and sold. Failure to comply with the terms of the statute
was punishable by forfeiture to the king of both the captor ship and its

[1] Marsden 1894 p. 254.
[2] This can be seen in the calendars of the patent rolls for the period.
[3] Stat. 2 Hen.V cap. vi.

prize and the imprisonment and payment of ransom by the master. The reason given for making these regulations was that people covered by truces and safe conducts of Henry V and his father had been killed and robbed on the high sea, in ports and along the coasts. Since, as has been said above, they were tried elsewhere, accusations of killing and wounding in the chancery petitions were more often incidental to attempts to recover goods than to their actual capture; but John Sampson of Plymouth, charged with committing treasons and felonies at sea, and receiving effective help in evading arrest (12), seems to be an example of the kind of offender whom the act was intended to discourage.

It was customary for a truce to provide for the appointment of conservators with special powers to punish truce breaking, but the severity of these regulations, and the fact that being statutory they remained in force after active hostilities had been resumed, were unprecedented. Their introduction was followed by a decline in the number of complaints of captures both in chancery and before the king and council, but their deplorable effect on the country's shipping was being stressed in parliament as much as twenty years later. There had been a protest in 1416 that the king's enemies overseas and in Scotland were breaking the truce with impunity since his subjects dared not retaliate for fear of the statute and this resulted in another enactment (4 Hen.IV stat. 2 cap. vii) allowing letters of marque to be granted to subjects who had been injured by truce breakers, provided that the truce did not expressly forbid their use.

Letters of marque and reprisal had long been a recognised sanction for the failure of the courts of one country to redress an injury committed by one of its nationals on the subject of another. The procedure in a maritime case in the fourteenth century was for the injured party to seek a remedy from the offender's sovereign, and if this was unsuccessful to apply to his own—in England to the king and council—who having assured themselves that justice had been withheld, issued an order to the officials of specified ports, for the arrest of goods of any member of the offending country up to the amount required to recompense the plaintiff. The proceedings were often lengthy, involving more than one approach to the foreign court and the exchange of several letters by the sovereigns before the letters of marque were awarded, and disagreement as to whether an injustice had in fact been inflicted or refusal to admit that an arrest was justified led to further claims and counter claims and could be a hindrance to foreign trade and a cause of international hostility. Truces of the fifteenth century forbade the use of the system, but it continued, and there are instances of it in operation among the west country petitions (15, 26, 66, 67) which suggest some of the complications to which it led. The 1416 statute was probably intended mainly to simplify the obtaining of these reprisals when they were permissible by allowing the injured party to make his complaint without formality the keeper of the privy seal, who would issue a letter to the offending power requesting redress. If this were ineffective the grant of letters of marque by the chancellor would follow.

Military campaigns alternated with negotiations leading to further measures being taken to control both official fleets and sea rovers of the west country, whose sea keeping activities had never ceased to cause complaints in chancery (18, 19, 21, 23, etc.). In 1426 a proclamation announced that goods captured at sea were not to be disposed of until the king's council or the chancellor or the admiral or his deputy had decided whether they belonged to friends or enemies.[1] A petition presented by Breton merchants in 1432 alleged that Devon captors were turning this order to advantage by bribing the admiral's deputy to empanel juries of their friends, who gave false verdicts that all that had been captured belonged to the enemy, which he put on record so that any subsequent commission of inquiry would find in favour of the captors (28). On the other hand, in 1435, the commons were petitioning in parliament that their seamen were suffering much damage because merchants in amity with the king were greatly benefiting enemy shipping by loading their cargo in ships of Spain and other hostile countries and, if they were captured, recovering any enemies' goods in them by producing false evidence. It was therefore decided that, for a period of three years, and saving any special treaty terms, goods of friendly nations taken in enemy vessels without safe conducts should be treated as lawful prize; and moreover the statute of 1414 was repealed for seven years because its terms were so harsh that the king's people were being discouraged from going to sea to safeguard shipping or to trade and the navy of the realm was seriously deteriorating.[2] But in spite of this and of the curtailment of the troublesome sea law protecting non-belligerents' goods, protests were again made, this time that English merchants and seamen were deterred from building ships since foreign merchants continued to recover goods captured in enemy ships by bringing suits to the king and council or the chancellor proved by false documents. In 1439 therefore, another act re-affirmed that friends' goods in an enemy ship could be seized unless the ship had a safe conduct.[3] Similar complaints in 1441–2 resulted in a further provision that safe conducts granted to the enemy or anyone else must be enrolled in chancery. In the same year the repeal of the statute of 1414 was extended.[4]

Whatever the state of shipping in general, the chancery proceedings show that merchants and shipowners had been putting armed vessels to sea from the western harbours before the treason statute was abrogated (e.g. 29, 30, 33, 37 etc.), and continued to do so in an increasingly well organized and extensive way afterwards. It is clear that groups of ships were regularly fitted out by the inhabitants of the surrounding country, often under the leadership of influential local men who had sufficient resources to risk being sued by allied foreigners or English merchants for refusing to restore captured goods—sometimes when the crews of the captor ships would have returned them (24, 75 etc.). The petitioners' complaints inevitably convey a one sided view and there is little in them to indicate the provocation given by the French and their supporters nor, indeed, the kind of ferocity that called for an order—proclaimed

---

[1] *CCR 1422–9* p. 264.
[2] Rot.Parl. IV p. 492; Stat. 14 Hen.VI caps. vii, viii.
[3] Stat. 18 Hen.VI cap. viii.
[4] Stat. 20 Hen.VI caps. i, xi.

among others in 1426—that captors bringing vessels and goods to land without their personnel must be arrested by the local authorities until they had ascertained whether their owners were friends or not, because crews of the enemy were usually brought ashore to be ransomed while those of friends were often thrown overboard.[1] The account of his sea keeping given by Robert Wenyngton of Devonshire, who was commissioned in 1449 to go in the king's service to clear the sea of robbers and pirates, has survived, and may be taken to illustrate the kind of incident which, on a much smaller scale, often lay behind the bald facts related in the petitions. Wenyngton with his well armed ' fellowship ' in a few small vessels, having taken two ships of Brest and caused other Breton ships to prepare to retaliate, fell in with a large fleet of ships of the Hanse, Flanders, Holland and Zeeland. He approached their admiral and, exercising a right claimed by Edward III for all English sovereigns, ordered him in the king's name to strike sail. The admiral refused, and when in consequence Wenyngton threatened to oversail him, he scoffed at the small English force and allowed his men to shoot at and damage the English ships. But when the latter, given a favourable wind, prepared to carry out their threat, the whole fleet surrendered, and went with Wenyngton and his fellowship to the Isle of Wight. He held them there while he notified the chancellor and council, claiming that the shooting had rendered the fleet forfeit to the king and that the damage to his ships would justify him in killing and drowning the crews unless otherwise instructed by the king and council.[2] The outcome is not recorded. The fleet belonged to countries which were not officially at war with England, and the renewal of hostilities during 1449 had brought defeat and the loss of nearly all the English conquests in northern France. Wenyngton's exploit was probably unwelcome as a danger to friendly relations with allied countries at a time when they were being fostered.

It may have been a reason for the re-enactment in 1450 of the statute of 1414. The terms this time were less severe: a defendant was to be attainted of treason only if he failed to appear after the issue of a writ for his arrest, and owners and victuallers would be liable to punishment only if present at the unlawful capture. There was also a provision giving jurisdiction over truce breaking to the chancellor with one of the chief justices as well as to the conservators. This jurisdiction was reaffirmed and elucidated in 1452,[3] but no increase in the chancellor's powers is discernible in subsequent west country proceedings. On the contrary from about 1450 petitioners began to ask frequently for offenders to be brought before the *king* in chancery, and this became the rule in requests after the accession of Edward IV in 1460. Foreign complaints of truce breaking practically disappear at this time. Active hostilities with France ended on land in 1453, though a formal truce was not completed until ten years later and then did not cover the high seas. French ships and ships trading with French ports continued to require safe conducts and

---

[1] *CCR 1422–9* p. 264
[2] Gairdner 1910 pp. 84 *ff.*
[3] Stats. 29 Hen.VI cap. vi, 31 Hen.VI cap. iv.

licences to trade until 1475, when a peace treaty was signed which expressly permitted the ships of each side to visit freely the ports of the other.[1] Until then English merchants and a few Bretons presented petitions to recover cargoes which had been captured in foreign ships. The complaints made after 1475 set out grievances of a complicated kind which would not have found a remedy elsewhere. The deposition of Henry VI is mentioned very occasionally when necessary to date a document and there is only one direct reference to an incident in the civil war between Lancaster and York (90).

The advantages which the judicial processes used by council and chancery had over those of the common law—freedom to cross county boundaries and enter franchises, the use of more effective measures to bring defendants into court and to ascertain facts and execute orders and judgements [2]—were particularly valuable in dealing with maritime offenders who, by the nature of their calling apart from any wish to escape, were hard to locate and might have little by which they could be distrained (cp. 17). It is difficult to say how successful the methods were. Clearly they did not eliminate long delays and the need for great persistence in tracking down goods and culprits often dispersed over many places; on the other hand a petition in chancery made speedy action possible to catch a defendant when for some reason he happened to be in court (e.g. 11, 44, 45a, etc.). There is some positive evidence of the recovery of ships and cargo, sometimes after long proceedings (e.g. 36, 55, 71), and when a succession of entries on the patent and close rolls concerning one case comes to an end without explanation it seems as likely that it was because some settlement had been reached as that the plaintiff had simply given up after the expenditure of much time and trouble.

Whatever their other advantages, suits in chancery were expensive (cp. 55d) and troublesome for both parties. To protect people from the damage of being brought to court by frivolous accusations a statute of 1363-4 provided that suitors must find sureties before the chancellor, treasurer and council to pursue their actions. The names of pledges to prosecute are entered on many of the petitions in the calendar, but do not appear on many others, depending perhaps on what earlier legal action had taken place. A statute of 1393-4 gave the chancellor power to award damages to defendants in suits in which petitioners failed to prove charges, and in 1436 it was enacted that before the granting of a writ *subpoena* the suitor must find mainpernors, i.e. sureties, who would undertake that the defendant would be satisfied for his damages and expenses if the complaint was not proved to be true [3] (cp. 40, 68). Mainprize, i.e. release on bail, by finding mainpernors who would undertake under a penalty of a large sum of money to produce the accused in court was commonly allowed to defendants who had been arrested.

---

[1] *Foed.* XI p. 508 XII p. 17
[2] Avery op. cit. pp. 133-5
[3] Stats. 37 Ed.III cap. xviii, 17 Ric.II cap. vi, 15 Hen.VI cap. iv.

NOTES ON EDITING

Each document or group of documents is headed with its serial number in the Calendar.

Each of these numbered items begins with the Public Record Office reference number, i.e. C1, which is the code for the class of Early Chancery Proceedings, followed by the number of each of the files, or bundles as they are called, into which the documents are made up, and the number of each document in its file, e.g. C1/7/195. This is followed by mention of the language of the document when it is not English, and a note of its condition: *damaged* or *badly damaged* indicates that words have been torn away; *words illegible* that there is defacement but no actual gap in the script. Words which have to be inferred are enclosed in square brackets, with a question mark where there can be nothing but a guess, and a blank where even this is impossible, e.g. in the case of a name or a number.

When the sense is ambiguous or the translation is very free, the words of the original are given in a footnote. Technical legal terms, such as the Latin names of writs, have been used only when they appear in documents and in the exact form of words found there.

The spelling of Christian names of English persons has been Anglicized and modernized where necessary. Surnames and all foreign names have been given in their original forms. Variations in the same name, when repeated in the same document, have been ignored.

Two of the items have been printed in full by W. P. Baildon in *Select Cases in Chancery*, (Selden Society Publications No. X), and several by C. L. Kingsford in *Prejudice and Promise in Fifteenth Century England*; in order that the collection should be complete these have been included in the Calendar either very briefly summarized or given in a more condensed form than the others.

The dates attributed to the petitions are those of the most likely term of office of each chancellor as given in *Lists and Indexes* Vol. XII p. vii. In many cases it has been possible to find supplementary evidence in the printed calendars of the patent and close rolls either from commissions and orders issued in connection with the petitions or from fortuitous references to the parties or other people and incidents mentioned in them. Although the dating of the rolls is not infallible, these entries can, as a rule, provide information not only as to dates but also as to the circumstances described in the complaints. Summaries of such information follow the documents to which they relate and have been used when possible to limit their dates. When the chancellor is not identified and other evidence is lacking or very doubtful the date is given as *uncertain* followed by the most likely guess.

C1/7/195 *French, damaged*

CHANCELLOR The archbishop of York

DATE 3 April 1388–4 May 1389

PETITIONER Fernando Alfonso of Lisbon, Portugal, foreign merchant, factor and attorney of Prince Edward, son of [the king of] Portugal.

COMPLAINT The petitioner had sold 600 lots[1] of figs and raisins in Dartmouth on 20 January 1386 to John Hunte, esquire, of South[ampton], John Rigulyn and John Colville, merchants of Plymouth, Devonshire, at 6s. 8d. the lot, amounting to 300 marks, [the goods to be delivered by?] the petitioner in fifteen days time, as appeared more fully in certain indentures made between them. He had delivered all the lots to John Hunte, John Rigulyn and John Colville in Plymouth [by 4 February as agreed and they had paid for them?] on the fifteenth day of the same month, and had made an agreement with the petitioner concerning 261½ of the 300 marks, which sum [he owed to a third party to whom he asked them to pay it? But they had not done so, alleging it was owed[2]] to a certain Myceloys, Lombard, and merchant of London, on behalf of the prince of Portugal.

The petitioner had not been able to obtain payment of the 261½ marks from John Hunte, John Rigulyn and John Colville although he had incurred great labour and costs in [proceedings?] against them for recovery of that sum. He had nothing with which to continue his suit, and was on the point of utter ruin[3] unless he had the chancellor's most gracious aid.

REQUEST That the chancellor would consider this matter and the petitioner's poverty and that he was at the time a foreigner in the noble realm of England without anyone to help him,[4] and provide and ordain a just remedy out of his wisdom and discretion, so that the petitioner should be paid the 261½ marks by Hunte, Rigulyn and Colville, as good conscience and reason required, for God and in the way of charity.

[1]*sortes*
[2]or failing to carry out the agreement in some other way which involved payment to the Lombard.
[3]*d'estre perpetualement destruitz*
[4]*sanz comfort socour et eide de nully*

Editor's Note. The last few words of each line of the manuscript are missing so that it is impossible to follow the petitioner's transactions with his three debtors with certainty. Described as master of the order of St. James of Portugal, he is on record in the patent and close rolls as being indebted to other merchants of London in 1385, when ships of Portugal were seized off Southampton by his English creditors and brought into the port. There they were arrested at his suit, and the mayor and others were appointed on his petition to sell the ships' cargoes and to satisfy his debts to the English merchants out of the proceeds. This brought him into trouble with the collectors of customs for not obtaining the necessary licence for the unloading and sale of the goods and not paying the customs due on them. He was, however, discharged of the offences and of payment of £68 14s. by order of the king, who had pardoned him because he had said he was ignorant of the customs regulations in force in the realm (*CPR 1385–89* p. 9; *CCR 1385–89* p. 22).

Not long afterwards a London fell dealer obtained an order forbidding another London citizen from paying to anyone £31 14s. 8d. which was in his hands, because it belonged to Alfonso, and he owed the fell dealer £32 for goods purchased. In the same way, Alfonso himself had earlier prevented two merchants of London from paying money they owed to a Spaniard for merchandise bought in Southampton since he had a claim against the Spaniard. The London merchants had to petition for an order to the mayor of the port to dearrest their ship which was being detained because of non-payment for the goods. This was granted on condition that they found security to pay the money they owed to whichever party it was awarded (*CCR 1385–89* pp. 5, 25).

For evidence that Fernando Alfonso undertook some service in Portugal for the English king *c* 1386, see below 5 note p. 5.

2

C1/6/193 *French, damaged*

CHANCELLOR The bishop of Winchester

DATE 4 May 1389–27 September 1391

PETITIONER Robert Stamford of Dartmouth, 'your poor diseased[1] subject'.

COMPLAINT The petitioner had gone recently with Walter Bachelor, the king's searcher in Dartmouth, and others at his request, to support him in searching a ship of Esmond Arnold, who was said to have disloyally evaded the king's custom on certain bundles of cloth and much other merchandise which he had loaded in the same ship for Portugal, as the petitioner was ready to prove by his body if the law allowed, or otherwise by good and sufficient proofs.[2] And Esmond Arnold with eight of his servants armed with axes, swords, bows, arrows and daggers, having lain in wait[3] in two boats, had feloniously and against the peace assaulted the searcher and wounded the petitioner in various parts of his body [so badly that] Esmond had left him for dead.

REQUEST That the chancellor would consider Esmond's great disloyalty at that time and appoint a day [in the king's chancery], and for punishment and as example to other evildoers send for Esmond by writ and then ordain that he be punished and his goods seized for a fine[4] for his disloyalty and horrid deeds, and that the [petitioner should receive] reasonable amends from him for his beating and wounds, for God and in way of charity, and he would pray devotedly for the rest of his life for the souls of all the chancellor's illustrious ancestors, and also for him.

[1] *desease*

[2] *est prest de faire bon sur son corps si le loy luy voudre a ce admettre ou outrement de le prover sur luy par bones et sufficeant proves.* The petitioner seems to be offering to prove his accusation by showing his wounds.

[3] *gesoit en agait*

[4] *mulcte par ses biens*

3

C1/7/251 *French*

CHANCELLOR The archbishop of York

DATE 27 September 1391–1 October 1394

PETITIONER John Elys of Winkleigh,[1] merchant.

COMPLAINT The petitioner had lately recovered £28 before the earl of Rutland, admiral of England, by judgement of his court, against John Sampson of Plymouth, the younger, and his pledges. Robert Beverle, a sergeant-at-arms, had been commissioned by the admiral to execute the judgement and had taken and imprisoned John Sampson; but the latter was now at large without having satisfied the petitioner for the £28. The petitioner could obtain no answer from the sergeant.

REQUEST That the chancellor would grant a writ to make the sergeant come before him to answer concerning the matter, for God and in way of charity. The petitioner would find security for his costs if this allegation were not found to be true.

[1] *Wincle*

Editor's Note. The earl of Rutland was admiral of England from 22 March 1391 until the following November (Nicolas 1847 II p. 531). The added reference to finding security suggests that this petition was presented soon after the passing of the act of parliament in 1393 which gave the chancery power to require a plaintiff to find pledges to guarantee the compensation of the defendant if he could not prove his allegations (see Introduction p. xviii).

John Elys had brought an earlier action of debt against John Sampson the younger in the maritime court of Lostwithiel, and had recovered £6 0s. 4d. out of goods seized by the officials of the court in a chest which John Sampson had brought to that port in a crayer of Brittany (Marsden 1892 I pp. 3ff. and 152ff. cp. also 6 and 12 below). The cause of the debt was not mentioned in either action, but since both judgements were given in the admiral's court the assumption is that they related to maritime matters, though this did not always follow: complaints were being made at this period that the court was exceeding its jurisdiction (Ibid p. 1).

4

C1/3/43 *French, printed in full by W. P. Baildon 1896 p. 45.*

CHANCELLOR The bishop of Exeter

DATE 23 November 1396–14 July 1399

PETITIONERS Henry Mayn and William Mayn his brother, merchants of Dartmouth.

COMPLAINT On 10 August 1391, in time of peace, the petitioners had loaded a ship called the *George* at Dartmouth with woollen cloth of various colours, alabaster images and other merchandise valued at one thousand pounds, intending to cross the sea towards Seville; and Piers Laurence, master of a ship of Genoa, had come, like a sea robber, with many others in league[1] with him and with force and arms seized the ship *St.*[*sic*] *George* and all the merchandise in it and carried them off to his own country, without making any recompense or restitution to the petitioners. On 18 June 1396, Henry Mayn had caused Piers Laurence to be arrested for this offence in Southampton and brought before John Botiller, then bailiff of that town, where he had been examined and had admitted and confessed the offence and had offered to compensate Henry and besought him to have grace and mercy. He had been committed to prison until next day, when the bailiff had brought him to the guildhall before John Flete, mayor of Southampton. Henry Mayn in full court had openly prayed and requested the mayor and bailiff, since it was their duty to enforce the king's laws there, to do him such right and law on the king's behalf as was ordained and appropriate to such an offender and wrongdoer since Piers had openly admitted and confessed the trespass. But the mayor and bailiff would award no remedy for the offence, but wrongfully, contrary to right and law, ordered two sergeants to keep Henry in prison in their guildhall until Piers Laurence had, with their connivance, escaped and crossed the sea, and so by their deceit and falsity the petitioners would lose all their goods for ever if a remedy were not ordained by the chancellor.

REQUEST That he would grant a writ directed to John Botiller and John Flete ordering them to be before him on a day to be given in it, to answer the petitioners concerning the matter, and to be examined as to the whole truth touching it, so that due remedy might be ordained on whatever was found by examination or confession, for God and in way of holy charity.

[1] *de sa covyne*

Editor's Note. John Botiller, bailiff of Southampton, was in trouble for allowing another prisoner to escape at about the same date (*CPR 1391–96* p. 707).

5

C1/69/309 *French*

CHANCELLOR The chancellor of England

DATE Uncertain, possibly 1390–1400

PETITIONERS Laurence Smyth of Fowey in Cornwall, Richard Stonard and John Russell, both of the same county.

COMPLAINT The petitioners recently had a ship worth £60 taking overseas various merchandise from different parts of the English coast.[1] They had one servant between them in the ship, John Pomeray, to buy and sell their merchandise. Philip Mayhowe, John Wilkok, David Russell, Sampson Chinals, Stephen Regenes, John Baker, Ronald and John Balard and others all of Fowey in the county of Cornwall, were men and boys in charge of the ship.[2] John Pomeray had bought salt valued at £60 in Brittany, at the petitioners' cost and put it in the ship to bring it to England for their use. As the ship was sailing for England it was met by several armed ships[3] of Normandy, and the crew were forced to turn it back; they came to the district of Leon between le Forne and St. Pol in Brittany. There Philip Mayhowe, John Wilkok, David Russell, Sampson Chinals, Stephen Regenes, John Baker, Ronald and John Balard took the ship and the salt in it and sold them to various Bretons contrary to the wishes of the petitioners.

REQUEST That the chancellor would make the men named come before him in the chancery to answer the petitioners in the matter and to do whatever was right, for God and in way of charity.

Pledges of prosecution: Robert Greyaga, Henry Bekerton.

[1] *passant sur le mier pour mesner divers marchaundises de divers parties de la mere en la Roialme dengleterre*
[2] *governoures et valetz en mesme la nief*
[3] *niefs ou gentz armes*

Editor's Note. The date of this petition is indicated only by references in the close and patent rolls to some of the men named in it. Richard Stonard was among those commissioned in 1432 to inquire into the complaint of John Brykles of London (cp. 29 below) but his is the only name to appear so late. Men named Laurence Smyth, John Russell and Johno Wilkk, connected with seafaring in the west country, seem to have been active between 1385 and 1403, i.e. John Wilkok was one of twenty named men who, in 1386, were delaying the sailing to Portugal on the king's service of Fernando Alfonso and his company, by wandering about the country finding excuses for not going with him although they had been retained by him and paid large sums of money (*CCR 1385–89* p. 65).

In 1393 Laurence Smyth and about forty other named merchants of Cornwall were pardoned, on payment of £200, for shipping tin overseas without taking it to the staple at Calais (*CPR 1391–96* p. 263).

Miscellaneous goods of John Russell and others were forfeited in 1397 because they were found uncustomed in various ships by the searcher in

Southampton. In 1403 he was involved with many others of Devon and Cornwall in the capture of Spanish ships (*CPR 1396–99* p. 116, *CCR 1402–5* p. 57).

6

C1/3/118 *French, printed in full by Baildon op. cit. p. 42.*

CHANCELLOR The bishop of Exeter

DATE June 1397–23 August 1399

PETITIONER John Charleton

COMPLAINT In the year 1397–98, the petitioner's ship, called the *Mary of Plymouth*, worth £200, loaded with various goods and merchandise of his own and of others in his keeping, valued at £200, had been sailing to Plymouth when William Benteley, then lieutenant of the king's admiral, arrested it by pretext of his office without reasonable cause, and brought it to Plymouth. There Stephen Derneford the elder, John Sampson the younger, Henry Crese and William Benteley, scheming to destroy the petitioner's estate, conspired together so that Stephen had affirmed a plaint of debt against the petitioner in his absence before Henry Crese, then water bailiff of Plymouth, for the sum of 500 marks which he was said to have received from a child, Denis,[1] to the use of Stephen. In confirmation of their conspiracy, John Sampson had forged an acquittance supposed to be from the petitioner to the child Denis proving the alleged receipt, whereas the petitioner had not received a penny from the child Denis, nor made any acquittance. Nevertheless, Henry Crese, the water bailiff, in the petitioner's absence and without due process of law, had caused the ship and all the goods in it to be appraised and delivered to Stephen for the said sum, except the sail, cables and other equipment which Henry Crese took for himself, claiming 12d. in each pound as his fee[2] in the said cause, wrongfully and contrary to law and right to the great damage of the petitioner.

REQUEST The petitioner sought a remedy, for God and in way of charity.

[1] *un enfant Denys* This is translated: " one, Child Denys " by Baildon but he expresses a doubt about the sense. It seems possible to interpret it literally as " child ", implying one too young to take part in the legal proceedings.
[2] As water bailiff. Cp. below 31, note p. 34

Editor's Note. Stephen Derneford and William Benteley were employed on the business of the crown in the west of England between 1385 and about 1408 without other accusations of malpractices, but John Sampson the younger was constantly being pursued for failing to appear to answer charges in courts of law during the same period. Although there is nothing to show it, John Charleton's complaint may have been among the many felonies and ' other extortions ' for which his arrest by William Benteley was ordered some time before the end of 1408 (See petition 12 below and Introduction p. xii).

7

C1/68/91 *French*

CHANCELLOR The chancellor of England

DATE 1400-4 or 1413-16

PETITIONER Thomas Patryk, subject[1] of our lord the king

COMPLAINT The petitioner with Michael, master of the ship *Jonet of Dart-mouth*, and John Bolt of Dartmouth, owner of the ship, and others lately in time of war between our sovereign lord and king and the Scots took goods and chattels valued at £3,000 of which the king ought to have one third. Because the petitioner would not agree to conceal this profit due to the king he was imprisoned at Haverford West and sent from there to imprisonment in Bristol and had been in prison for a year and more; and was still there because he could not find surety for £300 that he would never make a charge about the third part nor reveal their conspiracy concerning the said goods.

REQUEST That the chancellor would grant the petitioner a writ to show the cause of his arrest and detention[2] so that he be brought before him on a certain day to give a fuller declaration about this matter for God and in way of charity, and for the profit of £1,000 for the king.
At foot of document: A writ directed to the mayor and sheriff of Bristol *de habendo corpus cum causa etc.*

[1] *liege homme*
[2] *un breve de causa capcionis et detentionis*

Editor's Note. In the absence of the identity of both king and chancellor, and of any other record of the parties, the only indication of date in this petition is the reference to the war with the Scots. This was active at the beginning of Henry IV's reign (*CCR 1399–1401* p. 168 *CPR 1399–1401* p. 394). The Scots were also allies of the French against Henry V, with brief intervals of truce, from 1413 till 1416 (*CPR 1413–16* pp. 28, 273 etc. *CCR 1413–16* pp. 92, 268, 369).

8

C1/69/312 *French, some words illegible*

CHANCELLOR The chancellor of England

DATE 1404

PETITIONER Nicholas Bygge, poor seaman, master of a 60 ton barge, the *Trinity of Brixham*.

COMPLAINT The barge with 16 seamen had lain for seven weeks, and was still lying, under arrest for the king in the waters of the Thames[1] without wages or reward. During that time the petitioner had spent so much to keep his seamen together without leaving the barge, for the king's service and pleasure, that he had put most of the ship's tackle in pledge, to the utter ruin of his small estate if the chancellor did not provide him with a remedy.

REQUEST That he would consider his great distress[2] and that he had been without other means to keep his seamen together with no wages and would grant him, out of grace and wisdom,[3] wages to retain the crew or, alternatively, permission to go to Brixham with the ship for the king's service there, notwithstanding the arrest, for God and in way of charity; and taking into account[4] that otherwise he would suffer the loss of the barge because of his great indebtedness in the matter.

    [1] *Leawe de Thamise*
    [2] *le grant mischief et desease*
    [3] *de votre habundante grace et droiture*
    [4] *Entendantez*

Editor's Note. An order was issued to the mayor and sheriffs of London and the keepers of the passage and the searchers in the port on 3 May 1404 to allow Nicholas Bygge to take his barge on the king's service to Brixham. Similar orders were given at the same time to the masters of two crayers of Dartmouth, one under arrest in London and the other in Chichester to go to Dartmouth to carry on their own trade (*CCR 1402–5* p. 338).

9

C1/4/190 *French, damaged*

CHANCELLOR The bishop of Durham

DATE 8 August 1406–29 January 1407

PETITIONER Nicholas, factor and attorney of John Disco, merchant and burgess of the city of Pamplona in the kingdom of Navarra.

COMPLAINT Nicholas had presented a letter from the king of Navarra to the king of England praying for the restitution of 21 tuns of oil valued at fifteen hundred gold scudi of France, which had been taken at sea by people of Bristol and Dartmouth some two or more years ago. The oil had remained in the control of John Hawley and his son who were doing what they chose with it.

REQUEST That the chancellor would make John Hawley and his son do right and justice to Nicholas concerning the aforesaid sum and the costs and damages he had incurred during the past two years.[1]

    [1] *par luy faitz en temps passee*

Editor's Note. Olive oil owned by John Disco of Navarra was the cause of several orders and commissions between December 1403 and March 1407. Most, if not all, of them related to a cargo in a Spanish ship captured with a number of others by a fleet from Bristol and other west country ports under the leadership of John Hawley of Dartmouth and Thomas Norton of Bristol in the autumn of 1403 when a truce with Spain had just been concluded (*CPR 1401–5* pp. 360, 361, 363, 428; *CCR 1402–5* p. 257).

Although the date of the above petition could not have been earlier than 8 August 1406, when the bishop of Durham became chancellor, it almost certainly referred to this cargo. After capture it had been taken to Dartmouth and put into the custody of John Hawley and his son and a number of other men by consent of the crews of the whole fleet, who had evidently refused to accept whatever proof of Disco's ownership had been offered, since they had also agreed that a letter to him should be prepared in Bristol telling him what had been done and asking him to notify his factor there, Nicholas Yraycos, by a letter from the king of Navarra that the oil was his, whereupon it would be delivered to Nicholas. The king of Navarra had sent letters to the king of England certifying that the oil belonged to Disco, and John Hawley and the others were ordered on 6 March 1404 to deliver it or its price to Nicholas Yraycos (*CCR 1402–5* p. 267).

For some reason this was not done, as the above petition shows, either then or in response to further orders later in the same year (*CPR 1401–5* pp. 437, 507). Drastic steps were taken in March 1407 to bring John Hawley the younger into chancery. He had departed from the court without leave after appearing to answer concerning the capture of 14 tuns of Disco's oil, for which the king would have to make restitution if Hawley did not do so, and if it had, in fact, been taken during the truce (*CCR 1405–9* p. 177). Possibly Nicholas had received what was left of the oil in the Hawleys' custody as a result of his petition and this action was an attempt to recover the value of what had been dissipated in the meantime.

10a

C1/16/29 *French, badly damaged*

CHANCELLOR The archbishop of Canterbury

DATE 30 January–April 1407

PETITIONER John de Pynell, merchant of Lisbon in Portugal.

COMPLAINT In the previous August the petitioner and his barge, the *Marie de la Scale*, loaded with salt valued at 500 marks, had been seized at sea by two balingers, one of Fowey, of which John Gascoyn was master, and the other of Dartmouth, John Mayhew master, of half of which John Corpe of Dartmouth was partner and fitter out.[1] They had brought the petitioner with his barge and merchandise to the port of Shoreham, and there sold the salt, and did what they pleased with other things.

[The petitioner had sued earlier to the king and council] and sought that the king would grant letters patent to Thomas Wodevile, sergeant-at-arms, to cause just restitution to be made of the things and [compensation to be paid for the petitioner's costs?] and damages. The sergeant-at-arms had gone to Dartmouth and Fowey and arrested John Mayhew and John Gascoyn, on the strength of the commission, and afterwards released them on mainprise. [John Corpe had mainperned for John Mayhew, and had undertaken, and failed, to have him?] before the king and council fifteen days after the previous feast of St. Hilary,[2] to the great detriment of the petitioner, who had not yet obtained full execution of justice.[3]

REQUEST [That the chancellor] would cause justice to be done to him by John Corpe, who had received the greater part of the money for the sale of his goods and was mainpernor of John [Mayhew . . . and also by] the other plunderers, and to compel them and John Corpe to pay him the 500 marks and his costs and damages for God etc.

[1]John Corpe de Dertemuthe [. . .] parsoner et armendour de les deux parties
[2]i.e. on 28 January.
[3]nad ne poet avoir complement de justice

10b

C1/16/30 French, badly damaged

CHANCELLOR The archbishop of Canterbury

DATE April–July 1407

PETITIONER John de Pynell, merchant of Portugal.

COMPLAINT The petitioner had been sailing in his barge, Marie de la Scale, laden with salt and other merchandise valued at 500 marks, when it was seized at sea and plundered by two English balingers, masters: John Mayhew of Dartmouth and John Gascoyn of Fowey, and taken to Shoreham in England where the salt and other merchandise had been removed from the petitioner's possession. Three hundred and twenty-nine quarters of salt, valued at 10s. the quarter, totalling £164 10s., was in Shoreham in the possession of John Sculle, John atte Gate, Alexander Pynchon and Simon[1] Benefeld with the consent of the plunderers. And the four men had been put on oath, both by letters and messengers of lady Arundell and by the petitioner, to keep the goods and not to deliver anything to the plunderers until the right to the goods had been determined before the king and council.

REQUEST That the four men named should be compelled to restore the goods or their value to the petitioner with his costs and damages; and that the chancellor would please to consider that he had spent nine months in England on the matter and had no means to support him there any longer; and also that John Corpe—who had recently on his own confession been found by the chancellor both to have had most of the goods and merchandise and to have been mainpernor of John Mayhew—should be kept under arrest and not allowed mainprise until he had satisfied the petitioner in full, both on his own behalf and that of John Mayhew, for all the goods and merchandise and the costs and expenses, for God etc.

[1]Symkyn

Editor's Note. These two petitions were evidently part of proceedings which had been begun by a complaint from John de Pynell to the king and council. Several commissions relating to them are entered on the patent rolls, and another petition from him and a letter from the king of Portugal, both addressed to the king of England, are preserved among the Ancient Petitions. These documents show that John de Pynell's ship had previously been captured by Bretons and taken to Brittany where the cargo it was then carrying was disposed of by the captors. He had sought aid from the king of Portugal and supported by a letter from him, had recovered the ship and received compensation for the cargo by award of the court of the duke of Brittany. He had then reloaded the ship with salt at Guèrande and was on his way to Middleburg in Flanders from Brittany in August 1406 when he and his ship were again captured, this time by the two English balingers, and taken to Shoreham (PRO S.C.8 185/9211). There he and his companions had been imprisoned as enemy Bretons, and the ship and its contents taken into the possession of the captors as lawful prize (*CPR 1405–8* pp. 301, 357).

The reference to lady Arundell in the second petition above suggests that John de Pynell had asserted his nationality and offered some proof of his right to the ship and merchandise to the local authority at Shoreham, where the lords of Arundell presumably had jurisdiction. At all events he was released from custody after eleven days, and obtained the undertaking from those in possession of the salt not to release it to the captors until his claim to it had been adjudicated by the king and council.

The letters patent to which he referred in petition 10a were two commissions issued on his complaint: one, on 1 October 1406, addressed to the mayor of Fowey as well as to Thomas Wodevile, contained no reference to Bretons, but ordered that restitution should be made of ship and merchandise and that all who refused should be arrested and brought before the king and council with all speed. The other was issued on 31 December to Thomas Wodevile alone—following, it may be assumed, his failure to produce the defendants in court—and was identical with the first, but fixed fifteen days after St. Hilary for the appearance of those who refused to make restitution (*CPR 1405–8* pp. 301, 302). Again they did not appear as the petition 10a above shows. The latter was however followed eventually by the appearance of John Corpe. This can be gathered from petition 10b which was primarily concerned with taking action against the four men in possession of the salt of Shoreham, and produced another commission to Thomas Wodevile, dated 12 April 1407, ordering their arrest and appearance before the king and council (*CPR 1405–8* p. 350). There is no evidence that they appeared, but John Gascoyn did and pleaded that the ship and goods and merchandise belonged not to John Pynell but to the king's enemies of Brittany (Ibid. p. 357).

This defence was successful to the extent at least that John de Pynell was refused restitution until he had produced further proof of his claim. Two months or so later he presented yet another petition to the king, producing a letter from the king of Portugal which certified that he was a subject of that country and that the ship and cargo were his, and offering letters under seals of the mayors and commonalties of Bristol and Southampton and the testimony of reliable English, Gascon and Portuguese witnesses, and seeking an order to the chancellor to bring the case, and John Gascoyn and John Corpe and seven men of Shoreham, who had bought the goods, before the king. (S.C.8., 185, 9210, 9211). He was granted another commission, dated 17 July, to five men, not including Thomas Wodevile, ordering them to inquire by oath of good men of Cornwall and others into the capture of his ship and cargo contrary to the truces between the king and the king of Portugal (*CPR 1405–8* p. 357).

Whatever the outcome was of this, it seemed to close the proceedings. There are no further references to the case. There is however one more a year later to John de Pynell which may indicate some repercussion: two men of London undertook that he would be in that city until he had answered an unspecified court case brought by Simon Benefeld and other men of Shoreham (*CCR 1405–9* p. 386).

11

C1/69/60 *French*

CHANCELLOR The chancellor of England

DATE 1408–9

PETITIONER Richard Garner, merchant.

COMPLAINT John Hawley the elder of Dartmouth, whose soul was in God's keeping,[1] had been in debt to the petitioner during his lifetime for £200 as appeared more fully in John's written obligation. The petitioner had sued John Hawley the younger in the common bench, as administrator of the goods and chattels of John Hawley the elder who had died intestate. The administrator, scheming maliciously to bar the petitioner from his action, had proffered a release by which the petitioner, after the obligation had been drawn up, was supposed to have discharged John Hawley the elder from all manner of personal actions whereas he had never discharged him of anything. John Hawley the younger, persisting in his malice, in the name of John Hawley only, had sued the petitioner, also in the common bench, in the names of Richard Garner of Piedmont and Peter Kyng by a writ of trespass which alleged that they had taken by force and carried off from Fowey and Saltash in the county of Cornwall, goods and chattels of John's valued at £100 and £100 in money, of which they were innocent, and he had done it only to make the petitioner abandon his own suit.

Moreover, certain seamen and servants of John Hawley lately at sea in a ship of war of his, knowing the ill will he bore the petitioner, took 10 pipes of wine out of a Breton vessel which the latter had freighted with wines of La Rochelle to bring to London, and they had assaulted and ill treated the servant in the vessel at the time so that he despaired of his life. The seamen had also said that if the petitioner had been there they would have beaten the eyes out of his head.[2] In these circumstances the petitioner would be put to great loss and wrongs if he did not have the chancellor's aid.

REQUEST That the chancellor would consider carefully what had been stated, and make John Hawley, who was then present in the neighbourhood, come before him in the chancery to be examined there concerning the release and the suit of trespass and to answer there for the offences committed by his seamen and servants and for any other matter with which he should be charged; for God etc.

Pledges of prosecution: John Bermyngham, Thomas Haseley.

[1] *a dieu commander.* John Hawley the elder died at the end of 1408.
[2] *ils vorroient avoir batu les oueils hors de son test*

Editor's Note. This seems to be the only surviving petition addressed by Richard Garner to the chancellor, although there are several to the king and council among the Ancient Petitions. There are also numerous commissions and orders on the patent and close rolls relating to goods which, he alleged, had been unlawfully captured at sea during 1403 and 1404. Only one such entry was made after the death of John Hawley the elder. It was dated 18 April 1409—six weeks or so after the grant of naturalization to Garner who was therefore no longer ' of Piedmont ' and was described as ' of London '—and probably related to part of the complaint in the above petition. The mayor and bailiffs of Dartmouth were ordered to make restitution to Garner—if they were satisfied that it was his—of wine which had been bought by his brother for him at La Rochelle in ships of Brittany and taken at sea by men of Dartmouth (*CPR 1408–13* p. 55, *CCR 1405–9* p. 434–5).

12

C1/69/155 *French, damaged*

CHANCELLOR The chancellor of England

DATE After 15 September 1408

PETITIONER William Benteley and William Soper and other poor people who were being grievously persecuted by Peter Whiteley, maintainer of John Sampson.[1]

COMPLAINT John Sampson had lately been accused before the king of many outrageous treasons, felonies, and other extortions committed by him at sea in contempt of the crown, therefore William Benteley had been ordered and strictly charged both by the king and by a commission given to him by Esmond, late earl of Kent, then admiral of England, to arrest him wherever he could be found, local franchises notwithstanding. Benteley, with William Soper and others to help and support him, had gone to Peter Whiteley's house where John Sampson and his wife had taken refuge and were living at the time, and Peter, although he knew of [the order and the commission] had hidden them in his dovecot so that William Benteley should not find them, thus harbouring a felon of the crown contrary [to the king's command] and to the commission.

A long time later, Benteley, with others supporting him, found John Sampson in the town of Moretonhampstead[2] in the county of Devonshire, and arrested him there and brought him to the late admiral at great cost and trouble. Peter Whiteley, at the instigation of certain ill-wishers[3] was now grievously persecuting the petitioners and about forty-eight others, alleging that they had destroyed his house and his goods and chattels found in it, of which they were not guilty, and he was continuing to persecute and harass them on this account contrary to right and reason and to their great loss and damage unless they received the chancellor's aid.

REQUEST That he would consider the matter and grant a writ to make Peter Whiteley come before him in the chancery under a fixed penalty to answer in the above matter and to any other matters which should be brought against him on the king's behalf, for God etc.

Pledges of prosecution: John Grove, John Grysby, both of Plymouth.

[1] *les queux sont grevousement vexey pousuer et travaillez par un Piers Whiteley mentenor [de John] Sampson*
[2] *Moreton' en le counte de Devonshire*
[3] *maleveullantz*

Editor's Note. Edmond (called Esmond in error in the petition), earl of Kent, was appointed admiral on 8 May 1407 and was killed on 15 September 1408 (*CPR 1405-8* pp. 291, 323. Nicolas 1847 p. 533). Both William Benteley and John Sampson were active at this time (see petition 6 above).

13

C1/75/1 *French*

CHANCELLOR The admiral of England

DATE 1410-11

PETITIONER John Andrew, lately vice-marshal[1] of the admiralty court in Devonshire.

COMPLAINT The petitioner had had a warrant from the admiralty court in Devonshire to arrest Uden Gledyk, son of Henry de Gledyk of St. Pol de Leon in Brittany, on which authority he had arrested him in Exeter; and one, Roger Hakeworthy, had come and wrongfully with force and arms in contempt[2] of the admiral's court, had taken Uden out of custody. On the road he had threatened to wound and kill the petitioner in such a way that he had barely escaped with his life. He was now suing a fictitious action of trespass at common law by the king's writ against the petitioner alleging that he had wounded Roger's wife, the intention of the action being to make it impossible for him to complain or sue to the admiral.

REQUEST That the admiral would grant him a writ under a penalty of 40 marks addressed to Roger Hakeworthy, ordering him to come and appear before him in chancery on a certain day to hear and answer the charges which would be made against him, both on the king's behalf and on that of the petitioner, for God etc.

Pledges of prosecution: Edmund Arnold of Dartmouth, and Robert Grigge of the county of Devon.

[1]*vismarshall'*
[2]*en despite de votre court*

Editor's Note. Thomas Beaufort, knight, was admiral of England and chancellor from 31 January 1410 till 5 January 1412, with a few days break in June 1411.

14a

C1/3/131 *French, printed in full by Baildon op.cit.* p. 90

CHANCELLOR The archbishop of Canterbury

DATE 1412

PETITIONERS Richard Gilbert and William Carswell, owners and victuallers of the balinger, the *George of Paignton*, and Thomas Rake, master.

COMPLAINT The men in the balinger, *George of Paignton*, had lately taken at sea a vessel laden with certain tuns of wine belonging to the French, who were the king's enemies, and brought it within the body of the county of Devon to a place called Torbay Jetty.[1] Then John Hawley,[2] although aware that the men in the *George* had made their prize, caused two of his balingers to be arrayed in unlawfully hostile manner[3] with a hundred men or more, armed and arrayed for war, who, when they saw the vessel which had been taken by the men in the *George* and was within the body of the county, prepared themselves to fight, unlawfully, and so threatened the lives of the people in the vessel that they left it in fear of death and went ashore. Whereupon the wrongdoers, contrary to right and reason, seized the vessel and the wines in it and took them to Dartmouth to the terror[4] of the aforesaid people and of the whole neighbourhood and to the damage of £250 to the petitioners.

REQUEST That the chancellor would grant a commission directed to persons to be selected by him to hear and determine the trespasses above-said, for God etc.

[1]*le Getee de Torrebaie*
[2]Son of John Hawley the elder. Cp. above, 9 and 11 and below 15 and 16.
[3]*en manere de insurreccion*
[4]*a graund affraie*

14b

C1/3/130 *Latin*

Henry, king of England etc. to John Hawley of Dartmouth. Greeting.

The king commanded him to inspect the enclosed bill which had been produced in chancery by Richard Gilbert, William Carswell and Thomas Rake alleging that certain injuries and grievances had been lately done to them by him; and to cause due and speedy reparation to be made concerning the matters contained in the bill, lest Richard, William, and Thomas should have to complain to the king again about them.

And if there should be reasonable cause why John Hawley should not do so, then he should certify it under his seal to the king in the chancery wherever it should be on the octave of St. Hilary next, so that the king may cause to be done further whatever justice required.

Witnessed by the king at Westminster on the 20 December 1412.

Endorsed: The answer to this writ appears in a schedule sewn to these presents.

14c

C1/3/132 *Latin, the answer of John Hawley.*

Memorandum that baron de Carrew, John Hawley and many seamen and men of Dartmouth had their ships at sea in warlike manner to destroy the enemies of the king and the realm; near the coast of Brittany, they took a crayer whose masters and owners were Bretons and which was freighted with wine and merchandise of the French, the king's enemies. The seamen put six Englishmen on board to guard it and bring it and its cargo to Dartmouth. Afterwards—during a truce between the king and those of Brittany[1]—the Bretons killed four of the six Englishmen. Whereupon the balinger, *George*, with the men in it came and took the aforesaid prize and carried it off to Torbay with one of the six men in it. Later John Hawley and the others took it peaceably as their own goods and chattels and brought it to Dartmouth. There the aforesaid baron, John Hawley and the others as well as the petitioners in the said bill submitted themselves concerning the foregoing to the judgement, ordinance and arbitration of John Corpe and John Foxley, elected on behalf of the baron, John Hawley and the others, and of John Carswell and John Madecombe elected on behalf of the petitioners. And they judged ordained and arbitrated that the baron, John Hawley and the others should have one half of all the said wine, goods and merchandise and the petitioners should have the other half. To which judgement the petitioners agreed, and they had their half of the wines etc. in the town of Dartmouth.

[1]There were truces with Brittany in force between 1407 and 1411 (Ramsay 1892 I pp. 108, 118, 122).

15

Cᵢ/6/120 *French*

CHANCELLOR The bishop of Winchester

DATE 21 March–13 April 1413

PETITIONER Peter Gunsales, master of a Spanish balinger called *Seint Croice.*

COMPLAINT King Henry IV, father of the present king of England, had lately granted to John Rodegys of Seville[1] in Spain and to the petitioner a commission directed to Edmond,[2] bishop of Exeter, and Thomas, baron of Carrewe, instructing them to make restitution to John Rodegys and the petitioner of the balinger and its equipment and of 85 tuns of wine which John Hawley of Dartmouth, proctor and attorney of Margery of Coventry, had seized recently during the truce made between the king of England and the king of Spain[3] by virtue of a marque[4] granted to Margery upon the goods and people of the town of Santander in Spain. But notwithstanding the said commission, John Hawley was unwilling to make delivery of the balinger and equipment or of the wines and was detaining them against the form of the truce and right and reason, to the great damage of John Rodegys and the petitioner if a remedy were not decreed by the chancellor.

REQUEST That the chancellor would arrest John Hawley and charge and compel him to make restitution of the balinger and its equipment to the petitioner in as good condition as they were when taken, and of the freight for the 85 tuns of wine together with all the costs and damages sustained by the petitioner, according to the tenor of the commission and truce, for God etc.

[1]*Civile*
[2]*Esmond*
[3]A truce with the king of Castile and Leon had been made in 1410 and prolonged from time to time (*CPR 1408–13* p. 180 *CCR 1409–13* pp. 327–8).
[4]i.e: Letters of marque or reprisal. Cp. introduction p. xv

Editor's Note. Merchants of Santander had captured a ship and merchandise, valued at 1250 marks, owned by Margery, widow of John Russell of Coventry, and had refused, she alleged, to make restitution although she had frequently sought it. Authority to seize any ship and merchandise of any merchant of Santander had been given to all admirals and others in the king's realms, on 10 March 1412, as marque and reprisal, to be retained for Margery until her claim had been satisfied. Letters of safe conduct were, however, to be respected (*CPR 1408–13* p. 389).

The commission referred to in Peter Gunsales' petition was issued in November, 1412. John Rodegys had complained that the balinger, which had been laden at Lepe in Spain, had been forced by bad weather into Dartmouth on its way to London, and had been seized by John Hawley by virtue of the marque and reprisal, although it was not of Santander. The bishop of Exeter and Thomas, baron of Carrewe, were instructed to seize it and keep it and its wines in safe custody while making an inquiry into the matter, and if they found Rodegys' complaint to be correct, to restore the ship and cargo to him. If John Hawley objected they were to compel him to appear in chancery before the following Easter (*CPR 1408–13* p. 474).

Hawley must have appeared in chancery to defend his right to retain the barge long before Easter, since the bishop and the baron of Carrewe were ordered in January 1413 to make restitution at once to Rodegys of his wine and to Peter Gunsales of the ship, notwithstanding both the letters of marque and also a previous command to deliver balinger and wine to Margery or her deputy. This seems to indicate some conflict of opinion over the judgement. The decision in favour of the Spaniards was given to prevent any complaint of breach of the truce which provided against seizures of ships and goods as marque and reprisal. The following Easter was the date by which claims concerning captures at sea by both sides were to be settled by a tribunal set up for the purpose. (*CCR 1409–13* pp. 381, 403).

The *Seint Croice* and her wine, however, were still in Hawley's custody in April. He, himself, was given a definite order on the 13th—presumably in response to Gunsales' petition—to deliver the ship to the latter and to keep the wine until it had been valued by Thomas de Carrewe and the mayor of Dartmouth, after which he was to sell it at the best price he could, pay the freight agreed with Gunsales out of the proceeds, and keep the remainder until further order. On the next day he made a recognisance to the king for 500 marks to be levied on his property in Devon if he did not carry out the order within a month after Easter (*CCR 1413–19* p. 8, *CPR 1413–16* p. 35, *CCR 1413–19* p. 67). A commission to arrest him without delay and bring him before the king in chancery was issued to Thomas Carrewe, the mayor of Dartmouth, and one other man on 10 August. No reason was given. (*CPR 1413–16* p. 116). It may have been the final step in the case.

16

C1/6/123 *French, damaged*

CHANCELLOR The bishop of Winchester

DATE 21 March–13 April 1413

PETITIONER Robert Russell, merchant of Bristol.

COMPLAINT King Henry, father of the present king, had taken under his safe conduct by letters patent dated 20 April last for one year any ship, barge or balinger that the petitioner should load himself or by merchants, attorneys or servants in the regions of [Castile or Brittany] as was set out more fully in the safe conduct; on the strength of which the petitioner, by his attorney, had loaded the *Gracedieu of Brittany* (John Berthe, master), in Brittany with salt as was contained more fully in the charter made between the petitioner and John Pennock, merchant of Brittany.

As the ship was sailing towards Bristol a number of wrongdoers, servants of John Hawley,[1] well arrayed for war, came and took the ship and everything belonging to it and the master and the seamen, disregarding the safe conduct, and brought them to Dartmouth. The petitioner had many times shown to John Hawley and his confederates the safe conduct and charter and also letters under the seal of the mayoralty of Bristol testifying that the goods belonged to him; nevertheless John Hawley refused to make restitution of the ship and salt to the petitioner's complete ruin if he were not aided by the chancellor.

REQUEST That the chancellor would consider the matter and grant writs, one directed to John Hawley and another to the mayor of Dartmouth, ordering them to make restitution of the [ship], goods and other things under a penalty to be fixed by the chancellor, for God etc.

[1]John Hawley, son of John Hawley, cp. 5, 11, 14, 15 above.

Editor's Note. Henry IV had died on 20 March 1413 and the bishop of Winchester had taken office as chancellor next day. On 13 April in the same year, the day on which John Hawley had been ordered to return Gunsales' ship, he, with the mayor of Dartmouth, was ordered in response to Robert Russell's petition to release the *Gracedieu of Brittany*, its crew and its cargo of salt, any command of the king or his late father to the contrary notwithstanding, because the petitioner had produced in chancery the letters of safe conduct protecting any ship, barge or balinger of Castile or of Brittany with its crew, equipment and cargo which he or his merchants or servants should load overseas, the charter made between him and John Pennok, merchant of Brittany, and the letters under the seal of the mayoralty of Bristol proving his ownership. The *Gracedieu* was said to have been taken at sea by men of Dartmouth and to be under arrest there but no mention was made of servants of John Hawley (*CCR 1413–19*) p. 9 See above 15.

17

C1/6/290 *French*

CHANCELLOR The bishop of Winchester

DATE 21 March–5 September 1416

PETITIONER Richard Bokeland, citizen and merchant of London.

COMPLAINT The petitioner and John de Boys, merchant of Brittany, lately during the truce between the present king and the duke of Brittany, had agreed by certain indentures made between them to be associates for trade in all kinds of adventure,[1] and the petitioner had delivered £80 of good English money to the said John de Boys in accordance with the content of the indentures. John de Boys had now recently come into the port of Plymouth under the king's safe conduct and brought with him divers goods and chattels for trade. The petitioner dared not take proceedings for his apprehension[2] nor against the said goods and chattels without the chancellor's aid because of the safe conduct.

REQUEST The grant of a writ directed to the mayor of Plymouth and to the guardians of the port commanding them to arrest the goods and chattels of John de Boys and to keep them under arrest and safe custody until he came before the chancellor in the king's chancery to answer the petitioner concerning the matter, for God etc.; and for consideration by the chancellor that John de Boys was an alien and only visiting,[3] having nothing by which he could be justified in the realm of England except what he had in the port of Plymouth, and that without such a remedy or something similar the petitioner was without redress.

[1]*Compaignons par voie de marchaundie a tout manere daventure*
[2]*rien nose faire au corps le dit Johan* John de Boys was presumably not honouring the agreement.
[3]*passaunt*

Editor's Note. A Richard " Buklande " was one of the customs collectors in the port of London in June 1415 and Richard Bokeland was a commissioner in September of that year. John de Boys had been granted naturalization in July (*CCR 1413-19* pp. 210, 220, 221 etc. *CPR 1413-16* pp. 361, 409). A truce with Brittany, which had been made in June 1413, was proclaimed in 1415 (*CCR 1413-19* p. 281).

18

C1/5/119 *French*

CHANCELLOR The bishop of Durham

DATE 23 July 1417–25 October 1418

PETITIONERS Simon Heron and John de Ligne, proctors and factors of William Guyhomar, merchant of Plancoet in Brittany.

COMPLAINT It was admitted[1] that during the truces between the king of England and the duke of Brittany a ship of the port of Erquy, called *la Trinite*, master: John de Lannay, who had freighted it with $48\frac{1}{2}$ pipes of wine of ' deniou,'[2] with all its people and wines had encountered certain armed balingers which were said to have been, and in fact were, with Sir John of Arundell near the roadsteads of St. Mathieu[3] on Monday 6 June, and ship and wines were taken and brought to Falmouth and there discharged at the inn[4] of David Urban, lieutenant of Sir John, in the presence of the good people of the town who could testify to it.[5]

It was also admitted that the value of the petitioners' wine amounted to two hundred and ninety one nobles at the six nobles a pipe or more for which they could have sold it in their own country or in Normandy at the siege of Cherbourg.

And their expenses and costs in making this suit amounted to more than 40 nobles without the damages they had suffered.

REQUEST The grant of letters of commission directed to honourable and wise men of the neighbourhood to release the goods in whose-ever hands they were, or otherwise to make those who detained them appear before the king's council in eight days after the delivery of the commission.

Endorsed: That the council agreed that John Hert, bailiff of Penryn by Falmouth and John Aleyn of Penryn be commissioned to call before them the parties specified in the petition, and do justice in the matter. And that writs should be addressed to each of the persons of whom the petitioners had complained to be before the council on the octave of St. Hilary next to answer what shall be put to them at their coming, and to do and execute etc.

¹*que come il soit et est vray*
²*Denion in CPR 1416–44 p. 204*
³*les chanaux de Seint Mathe*
⁴*en lostell*
⁵*qi bien purront dire la verite*

Editor's Note. The commission was issued on 25 October 1418 to John Hert and John Aleyn in the terms set out above (*CPR 1416–22* p. 204). There is however no record of the writs to the persons complained of in the petition; since the facts in the petitioners' complaint were not in dispute the wine was probably recovered without need for further proceedings.

Sir John Arundell, deputy to the admiral, was in command of a fleet for the protection of the southern seas during the summer of 1417 (Nicholas, op. cit. p. 436).

19

C1/4/29 *French*

CHANCELLOR The bishop of Durham

DATE May 1419–July 1424

PETITIONER Gyles de Taville, merchant of Algarve in the realm of the king of Portugal.

COMPLAINT That the petitioner had recently loaded 5 tuns and 1 pipe of his own wines among the wines of other merchants at la Rochelle in the barge *St. Katherine of Spain*, master: Martin Rodriges, Spaniard. As the barge, loaded with wines of la Rochelle, was sailing near Belle Ile it was taken by Sir John Ratcliffe, constable of Bordeaux, and others of the English fleet and brought to the port of Fowey in Cornwall and there sold by the constable and his deputy, wherefore the petitioner would lose his goods unless he had the chancellor's aid in this matter.

REQUEST Consideration by the chancellor that the petitioner was Portuguese and a friend of the realm of England and the grant of the necessary writs¹ directed to the constable and his deputies in England ordering them on the king's behalf to satisfy the petitioner for his goods loaded in the barge, for the saving of his poor and lowly estate, for God etc.

¹briefs busoignables

Editor's Note. Sir John Ratcliffe held the office of constable of Bordeaux from May 1419 until 1423. There are frequent references to him on the patent rolls at this time. (Vale, 1970; p. 247, *CPR 1422–29* pp. 124, 264, etc.)

20

C1/6/242 *French, fragment only*

CHANCELLOR The bishop of Winchester

DATE 1413–1416 or 1424–1426

PETITIONER William Benteleigh and John Horwode, both of Plymouth, and Thomas Warr.

COMPLAINT The petitioner had loaded the *Marie of Morlaix* with wine and it had been taken while under safe conduct by Nicholas Joop, John Petyte [. . .] Scarlet, Ralf Colyn and Reynold Touker . . . *nothing else legible except*: Pledges of prosecution: John Assh, John Copleston.

Editor's Note. The bishop of Winchester was chancellor both during 1413 to 1416 and 1424 to 1426. William Benteley [*sic*] was lieutenant of the admiral in 1397–8 (6 above) and presented petition number 12 *circ.* 1408. Probably it was the same William Benteley who was appointed a collector of customs in Plymouth and Fowey in 1421 (*CPR 1416–22* p. 392). John Copleston and John Copleston the younger were men of some standing in Devon between 1413 and 1422 (*CPR 1413–16* pp. 148, 354. Ibid. *1416–1422* pp. 159, 263, 403, 435 etc.).

21

C1/7/119 *French*

CHANCELLOR The archbishop of York

DATE March 1426–February 1432

PETITIONER Symon Rydoul, merchant, living at Bouchoir¹ near Amiens.

COMPLAINT The petitioner had loaded a ship of Dunkirk lately with six tuns and one pipe of woad.² On the previous 12 January a number of unknown robbers and wrongdoers of Holland had taken the ship and woad on the high sea and brought them to the port of Fowey in Cornwall, where they had delivered the woad to John Smyth, of Fowey, a merchant, on 16 May. Later the petitioner had brought the esteemed letters of the high and mighty prince, the duke of Gloucester, directed to John Smyth reciting that the petitioner was a subject of the king, and that the woad was his and wrongfully taken as stated above, and ordering John to make delivery of it to him. But John would not do so, and had still not done so; and before the 25 May last at Fowey had caused several persons unknown to take the petitioner in order to throw him in the high sea near the port. They took him on the said 25th day on to the sea in a ship which had been in the port, and had detained him there for the whole day until, in fear of death, to save his life and against his will, he made a document of release of all manner of actions to the wrongdoers who had taken the woad on the high sea.

REQUEST Consideration by the chancellor that he was a foreign merchant and could not stay in this country to suffer the delays of the common law in this case without the total loss of his merchandise, and that he was unable to sue the said John at common law concerning the matters in this case; and that the chancellor would cause restitution and amends to be made to him for the aforesaid trespasses, for God etc.

[1]*Bouchoure*
[2]*wode*

Editor's Note. Humphrey, duke of Gloucester, was protector of England during the minority of Henry VI from 1422 and was authorising letters patent until February 1432 (*CPR 1429–36* p. 155). The archbishop of York ceased to be chancellor at about the same time.

22

C1/7/126 *French*

CHANCELLOR The archbishop of York

DATE March 1426–February 1432

PETITIONER Jaqes Quateroilles, merchant, native of and living in Lisbon in the kingdom of Portugal.

COMPLAINT The petitioner had been accustomed to come to England with various merchandise, and had loyally paid his customs, and recently, i.e. on the first of May, he had come to Dartmouth, and was there arrested by John Foxlegh, Hugh Iyon' and John Berdwyk as deputies of the admiral of England, who put him in the custody of Robert Gybon, inventing law suits against him[1] to make him lose his goods and merchandise, to his utter destruction.

REQUEST That the chancellor consider the matter, and also that he was a subject of the king of Portugal, and grant him a writ directed to Robert Gybon to produce him with the cause of his arrest,[2] and three other writs of *subpoena*[3] directed severally to John Foxlegh, Hugh Iyon' and John Berdwyk to appear before the chancellor in the king's chancery on a day fixed by the chancellor to answer the petitioner concerning the matter, for God etc.

¹*imaginant causes sur le dit suppliant*
²*davoir le corps de dit suppliant oue la cause de son arrest*
³*briefs de sub pena*

Editor's Note. The John Foxlegh who was complained of above was probably the John Foxley [*sic*] who was one of the arbitrators for John Hawley and Baron de Carrew and others in 1412 (above 14c). John Foxley of Dartmouth was accused of assault and battery in 1423 (*CPR 1422–29* p. 137). He was also appointed with John Hawley esquire and others in 1431 to arrest ships and goods taken at sea and brought to Dartmouth, Fowey and Kingsbridge contrary to the peace treaty with France and to restore them to their owners (*CPR 1429–36* p. 127).

23

C1/7/95 *French, damaged*

CHANCELLOR The archbishop of York

DATE March 1426–February 1432

PETITIONERS Merchants of Spain.

COMPLAINT The petitioners had sued for a long time and at grievous expense for a ship and merchandise taken by certain people of Exmouth while under the king's safe conduct. The duke of Exeter had commanded that restitution should be made of all the goods and merchandise, and had sent his marshal with the petitioners to that part of the country and they had found their barge at a town called Teignmouth near Exeter. The marshal had arrested the barge and apprehended one of the victuallers who had been at its taking; and after his arrest it was said to the marshal and merchant [*sic*] that he pledged himself to return to the house of the baron de Carrewe¹ who lived three miles from the place where the arrest was made. On their way to the baron de Carrewe's house they had encountered about fifteen or sixteen people of Teignmouth who had attacked them and thrown them from their horses and taken the merchant into a wood and intended to kill him by cutting off his head,² and there came one, [name illegible], and demanded that he should give an acquittance of his claim to save his life or else he would never escape, and in terror of his life he answered that he would do all they wished. The following day they brought him before the baron de Carrewe, and before one called William Vynaert who had had most of the petitioners' goods and merchandise and kept them, contrary to all the orders; and the baron de Carrewe took him before a bishop to give the promised acquittance.³

REQUEST That the chancellor should do right and justice in this matter in way of charity. And that he would take into account that the names of those who took the said barge were: Nicholas Dandy, master, Payn

Dexemuth, [*sic*] victualler, John Payn of Exmouth, Bernard Gavon, Robert Milward, John Canon 'blake' of Teignmouth, John Bertons of Exeter, victuallers.

[1] *apres larrest fait lors fuist dit a dit Marchal et au marchant qil luy pleussoit aretourne par l'ostel de baron de Carrewe*
[2] *et le tenoient iusqes a la mort et luy voillent coupir sa teste*
[3] *pour doner quitance celluy quil pluist*

Editor's Note. The archbishop of York was chancellor from September 1391 to October 1394 as well as from March 1426 to February 1432. References to the duke of Exeter and Thomas de Carrewe favour the later date for the above petition (*CPR 1422–29* pp. 405, 550, 562, etc.)

24

C1/20/18 *Some words illegible*

CHANCELLOR The archbishop of York

DATE 29 April 1430 to July 1432.

PETITIONER John Lovell of Dundee in Scotland, merchant.

COMPLAINT On the 30 July in the year of our lord 1427, during the truce between the realms of England and Scotland, the petitioner was in his vessel off the harbour of Oleron(?)[1] in the sea of France, when John Hawley of Dartmouth, esquire, came with many others unknown to the petitioner with a large English fleet[2] and took him and his vessel and plundered him[3] there of goods and merchandise valued at £220.

The petitioner had sued a bill before the chancellor and the lords of the council, who had granted him a commission to the earl of Huntingdon for the arrest of John Hawley. The latter had then come to the petitioner and treated with him, excusing himself from responsibility for the taking and plundering, and promising and undertaking to satisfy him for his loss if he would get a commission directed to Hawley himself to arrest 40 or more persons. The petitioner had obtained three separate commissions from the chancellor and the lords of the council, addressed to John Hawley and others to whom he had consented, to arrest all the people he had specified whose names were given in the commissions. These Hawley had received and had arrested a number of people, so the petitioner was informed, and had taken large sums from them, but had not brought any of them before the chancellor to the petitioner's great hindrance and damage.

REQUEST That the chancellor would consider that he had been definitely informed that John Hawley had a great part of his goods and merchandise, i.e. the sail of the vessel, which he had given to [. . .], and 180 bars of iron[4] which had been in John Clement's house, and had been taken away by Henry Martyn of Kingswear, and wine and many other things.

The petitioner asked the chancellor to cause John Hawley to be condemned to satisfy him for the value of his goods and for reasonable costs and damages at the chancellor's discretion, taking into consideration that a number of the people of the fleet had offered to raise[5] between them 20d for every person of every ship to compensate the petitioner for his wrong and damages, which would have amounted to 1400 crowns [6] and more; or else to have satisfied him with £30 which John Hawley was holding of their own gold which was additional to their shares,[7] [and owed to them] for prisoners taken by the fleet valued at 2000 crowns.[8] But John Hawley had refused this offer. Therefore the chancellor could well understand that it was Hawley who was the cause of the petitioner's great hindrance, loss, costs and inconvenience,[9] and he asked him to consider these matters for the [love of God etc.].

[1] *before the havene of Ullon*
[2] *a grete navey of Ingland*
[3] *hym dispoiled*
[4] *yre*
[5] *to haf residde*
[6] *ml and cccc skutes*
[7] *over alle hire cantes*
[8] *ml ml skutes*
[9] *desese*

Editor's Note. The commissions mentioned by John Lovell in this petition can all be found on the patent rolls, and they limit its possible date. Thomas Carrewe, knight, and four others had been commissioned on 16 November 1428 with the earl of Huntingdon to arrest John Hawley of Dartmouth, esquire, and bring him before the king and council. Thomas Carrewe was also on the three commissions issued to John Hawley at John Lovell's request. Two other men were also included: one was the sheriff of Devon who was on commissions dated 9 December 1428 and 23 February 1429, but not on the third, issued over a year later in April 1430. All the commissions ordered the arrest of a number of named men, who were to be brought before the king and council or, in the second, the king in chancery. Thomas Buk, John Clement, Henry Martyn and three others were included in the first and the last, and the total number to be arrested was forty as John Lovell stated in the petition. (*CPR 1422–29* pp. 548, 549, 550. Ibid: *1429–36* p. 73).

25

Ci/8/14 *Some words illegible*

CHANCELLOR The archbishop of York

DATE November 1430

PETITIONER John Lovell, merchant of Dundee in Scotland.

COMPLAINT On the 30 July, in the year of Our Lord 1427, Thomas Buk of Dartmouth with many other persons unknown in the boat of their ship, of which Thomas Buk, was captain, owner and victualler, came aboard the petitioner's ship off the [harbour] of Oleron[1] in the sea of France, and plundered it contrary to the truce between England and Scotland and took it away from the petitioner with merchandise in it valued at £220. Afterwards Thomas Buk offered up the standard with the arms of the king of Scotland, which he had taken out of the ship, in the chapel of St. Petrox outside the castle of Dartmouth, as had been recorded and proved. And, in further evidence of the truth of the matter,[2] Thomas Buk had confessed in the presence of the baron of Carrewe that he himself was the leader[3] who had shared out the goods, for which wrong he had offered several times to satisfy the petitioner in part; but the latter would not agree, demanding the full value of the ship and goods from him since he had been the principal taker and disposer of the ship, valued as above said at £220: and the petitioner had incurred £100 expenses in making various suits and had sustained damages amounting to £100: total £420.

REQUEST That the chancellor would compel Thomas Buk, who was present in chancery at the time,[4] to make restitution to him of the aforesaid £420, according to the terms of the truce between the gracious and sovereign prince, the king of England, and the king of Scotland, and to do justice to him [in accordance with] the statute of [Lei]cester since he had acted against the truce of the gracious and excellent prince, for the love of God etc.

Latin Memorandum: That on 25 November 1430 Thomas was dismissed from the court [several words illegible].

[1] *h[aven]e of Ullon*
[2] *mor[over] for to have credence that this matter is sothe*
[3] *fourtheman*
[4] *the whiche is present here at this tyme*

Editor's Note. Thomas Buk was among the wanted men named in the commissions issued to John Hawley at Lovell's request. He was in chancery on 25 November 1430 giving an undertaking, under a penalty of 100 marks, not to do or cause to be done any harm to John Hawley of Dartmouth. Three " gentlemen " of different places in Devon and one of Dorset mainperned for him under a penalty of £20. The following day John Hawley gave a similar undertaking in regard to Thomas Buk. The mainpernors were Thomas Hawley of Dartmouth, gentlemen, two other "gentlemen" of Devon, and one of Cornwall (*CCR 1429–35* pp. 103, 104).
     Whether or not these undertakings related to some disagreement between John Hawley and Thomas Buk concerning the capture of John Lovell's ship and goods, they probably accounted for Buk's dismissal from the court before the judgement requested by Lovell could be passed on him. At all events another commission was obtained by Lovell a year and half later to Philip Courteney, knight, Nicholas de Carrewe, knight, five others and the sheriffs of Devon, Dorset and Cornwall. They were instructed to inquire into his complaint that certain wrongdoers of those counties had plundered his goods, valued at £220, and caused his ship to be cast away contrary to the truce; and to cause restitution to be made of the goods or their value and of the value of the ship (*CPR 1429–36*, pp. 197–8, 12 July 1432).
     No further specific references to the complaint have been found but an

order to arrest Thomas Buk and bring him before the king in chancery was issued to the mayor and bailiffs of Dartmouth and a sergeant-at-arms in August 1433 (Ibid p. 303).

26

C1/20/19 *Many words illegible.*

CHANCELLOR The archbishop of York

DATE 12 September 1430–25 February 1432

PETITIONERS John Caryewe, master of the *Mary of le Conquet*[1] in Brittany and John au Neste, master of *Saint Dulpholl of Abervynges* in Brittany.

COMPLAINT The petitioners had entered the port of Penzance in Cornwall on 12 September 1430 with their ships loaded with salt—one in the lordship of the earl of Warwick and another in the port of St Michael's Mount in lady Schyve's[2] lordship. Richard Tre[vense? b]ailiff of the earl, Martin Tregilliov, John Nichol, ' hurler,' tenants of the earl, and lady Schyve were the owners of the salt and they paid the petitioners well and truly for its freight. Afterwards John Caryewe had bought eleven dozens of cloth, i.e.: 8 dozen russet and blanket, and 3 of colours in whole dozens and remnants,[3] and loaded them in his ship the *Mary of le Conquet*, whereupon a number of men of the neighbourhood i.e.: Peter[4] Mynnov, John Willagooby, John Gatyn, Robert Mynnov of Marazion, Peter[4] Champyon, Martyn Hogekyn, Martyn Coseyn, Thomas Exion with their fellows,[5] and William Rosy of Mousehole[6] and his fellows,[5] had come and taken the petitioners' ships and cloth in warlike manner contrary to the truce between the king and the duke of Brittany, and kept them. Later John Mixstow of Fowey and Harry Nanskaseke of Truro had caused the ship and cloth to be arrested by the admiral's deputy, John Moure, by virtue of letters of marque granted by the duke of Brittany to Harry Nanskaseke's father nineteen years earlier; and they were keeping the ships and cloth to the great hindrance and undoing of the petitioners.

REQUEST That the chancellor would have a writ directed to the sheriff of Cornwall to proclaim that Breton merchants could at that time come and go safely to trade in accordance with the truce and also a writ of *subpoena* directed to John Moure, John Mixstow and Henry Nanskaseke to appear before him[7] to be examined concerning the letters of marque in reverence of God etc.

[1]*Conke*
[2]unidentified
[3]The term was used then as now for the ends of pieces of cloth.
[4]*Perys*
[5]*felaus*
[6]*Mousoll*
[7]*com in answer afore zow*

27

C1/45/14

CHANCELLOR The bishop of Bath

DATE 4 March 1432–13 May 1443

PETITIONER Richard Beauchamp, merchant of the isle of Guernsey.

COMPLAINT The petitioner had recently loaded 4 bundles of crese[1] cloth, valued at £40, in a pinnace of Brittany for Guernsey. It had been taken on the coast of the island by William Kydde and others in league with him, as appeared more fully in various records which the petitioner was ready to produce. It had been led away to Dartmouth, where it and the goods had been distributed in such a way that the petitioners doubted if restitution could be obtained from William Kydde. It had come to his knowledge however that the goods were in the hands of Robert and John Abbot, owners of the captor ship, from whom he could not obtain restitution without a remedy from the chancellor.

REQUEST That the chancellor would consider the foregoing and grant the petitioner writs of *subpoena* to Robert and John Abbot directing them to appear before him in the king's chancery to be examined concerning the matter, for the love of God etc.

[1]Coarse?

Editor's Note. Three men of the island of Guernsey made a complaint in 1430 against William Kydde that he with many others in his balinger had seized a ship near the island which the complainants had loaded in Brittany with supplies for the islanders. He was named again in 1431, but not as leader, among others who had captured ships of Rouen and Brittany. Described as of Exmouth, seamen, he with Robert and John Abbot, merchants of places in Dorset, and many others of south-west England were accused of attacking and carrying off a ship under safe conduct from a Breton harbour in 1435 (*CPR 1429–36* pp. 127, 128, 608. Ibid. pp. 83, 535).

28

C1/11/45 *French*

CHANCELLOR The bishop of Bath

DATE 4 March–5 June 1432

PETITIONERS John Donnart and Merian Pascu.

COMPLAINT To show the chancellor how well protected the wrongdoers on the sea-coasts of Devonshire were[1]: when they had taken any vessel or goods or merchandise of the king's friends, they sent at once for the deputy of the admiral of England and induced him to empanel a jury of 24 or 12 men who were for the most part relatives and friends of the same wrong-doers and the victuallers and owners. They gave their verdict that vessels, goods and merchandise taken from the king's friends belonged to the king's enemies, and then the wrongdoers caused the deputy to be in league with them,[2] and to enrol and record the verdict so given, by giving him half of the goods and merchandise for his trouble. In this way they made the king's commissions ineffective.

The petitioners said that the deputy who was thus in league with these wrongdoers would always be their guarantee, and this protection would always encourage[3] them to break the truces made between the king and his friends to the great damage of the petitioners and many others of the king's friends if the chancellor did not provide a remedy.

REQUEST They prayed the chancellor to consider the foregoing and how certain goods and merchandise of theirs valued at £250, taken by Robert Berewyn, Thomas Pedder and others of their confederacy, were in the hands of Thomas Pedder and Thomas Hamond the elder, John Hamond, Thomas Hether, William Scut, John Dyche, John Babbe, Walter Molton and John Swete; and that the petitioners had no remedy at common law to recover their goods and merchandise; and graciously to grant writs addressed to each of the above named men to appear before him in chancery on a certain date, under a certain penalty to be examined on the matter and to do all that reason and good conscience demanded for God etc.

Pledges of prosecution: Richard Burgh, John Sprotley.

[1]*Monsterount a votre gracious seignour de quel gouvernaunce sount les malefasours en la Countie de Devonshire par les costes de le meare*
[2]*destre de lour covyn' et assent*
[3]*mes diom que le dit depute quest de loue covyn' et assent serra toutzjours lour garant le quel governaunce toutzjours susteignera les ditz malefaisours*

Editor's Note. On 5 June 1432 Nicholas Carewe, knight, John Copleston, John Laurence, Richard Holand, John Hull, and Richard Cook, mayor of Exeter, or two or more of them, were commissioned to inquire in Devonshire and Cornwall as to the wrongdoers who took 135 pieces of linen cloth called ' cresecloth,' 4 pipes of Rochelle wine and other merchandise valued at £241 13s. 4d. belonging to John Donnart and Merian Pascu, merchants of Brittany, at sea in a ship, *le Skafre* of Kargonet, contrary to the peace between the king and the people of Brittany.

This was followed in August by another commission to Nicholas Carewe, John Copleston, and the mayor of Exeter (this time called William Cook), John Hull, Roger Burgh and John Baron, or two or more of them, to inquire into the alleged seizure of the same ship of Kargonet in Brittany and the same merchandise by Thomas Pedder, master, Robert Berewyn, and eight others, owners and victuallers, of a balinger of Teignmouth. The ship and goods were said to have been taken to Teignmouth and offered for sale there (*CPR 1429-36* pp. 218, 221).

This commission resulted in the discovery of the goods in question and their recovery by their owners. It also led to a complaint of extortion against John Baron (Below: 36 p. 39).

29a

CI/70/103 *Many words illegible*

CHANCELLOR The lord chancellor of England

DATE February 1432–November 1433

PETITIONER John Brykles, draper of London.

COMPLAINT In the previous December a ship [of Brieux in Britt]any [called *Saint Guille*, master: John Themovy, had been freighted by the petitioner's servant?] Robert Galos, to go from there to the port of London. While it was on the sea near the coast of [. . .]eal [Isle?] in Brittany, [William Chattoy, owner, and John Mestowet] of Fowey, victualler, and others in league with them, in a balinger called the *Magdalene of Plymouth*, armed and arrayed for war, [had captured] the ship and its cargo and taken it to Fowey. Fifteen tuns of wine in the ship [in Robert Galos' charge] had belonged to the petitioner. William [Chat]toy and John Mestowet [had imprisoned] John Galos, keeping him fettered and in irons for 6 weeks and 3 days, and forced him to acquit them of the capture.

REQUEST That the chancellor [would consider the foregoing] and grant the petitioner writs under reasonable penalties addressed to William Chattoy and John Mestowet commanding them to appear before him on a day fixed by him, so that the matter could be examined and a remedy provided in accordance with his wise advice and discretion in [way of?] charity etc.

Pledges of prosecution: Robert Saltmarsh and John Clerk, esquires.

29b

CI/9/393 *French, some words illegible*

CHANCELLOR The bishop of Bath

DATE 4 March 1432–November 1433

PETITIONER John Brykles of London, merchant.

COMPLAINT The petitioner had recently freighted fifteen tuns of wine in a barge, the *Seint Guille* of Brieux[1] in Brittany, to come to the port of London. Laurence Boy, lately of Fowey, dutchman,[2] Everard Ducheman, Robert Hull of Hull, Edmond Boteler of [. . .]an, with many others unknown, armed and arrayed for war, in a balinger, *le Magdalene*, of which Laurence Boy was master and owner, had come on 1 January 1432 on the high sea between the coasts of Brittany and England and despoiled the petitioner of the fifteen tuns of wine. They had also captured Robert Galloys, his servant, and taken him with the barge, the 15 tuns of wine and other wines and merchandise in it, to the port of Fowey in England and there delivered [and sold them to?] their confederates, victuallers, receivers and maintainers.

Of the petitioner's fifteen tuns of wine, six, amounting [to £20], had come into the possession of John Bodyer, merchant in the county of Cornwall appearing now before the chancellor in the king's chancery. This the petitioner had proved and was still ready to prove;[3] it had also been found by several inquiries held in the port of Fowey at various times.

REQUEST That the chancellor would consider the damage, loss and costs which the petitioner had sustained in the matter and do him justice in accordance with his most wise discretion and to cause restitution and due remedy to be made for God etc.

[1] *Bruys*
[2] *doucheman*
[3] *et unquore est de prover*

29c

C1/9/195

Memorandum of a declaration by Thomas Treffrye of Fowey in the county of Cornwall, gentleman, that on 10 November 1433 in the king's chancery at Westminster by assignment of the bishop of Bath, chancellor, Thomas Treffrye was sworn solemnly upon the book before John Frank, clerk of the rolls, to acknowledge the truth of that which he would be examined about at the request and suit of John Brykles of London, merchant, who had sued a writ of pain of £100 against Thomas Treffrye for 15 tuns of wine taken in a vessel of Brittany by Laurence Boy and others in league with him and brought to the port of Fowey; and that he, Thomas—examined by the said clerk of the rolls as to whether any pipe, tun or hogshead had come into his possession or keeping, or if he had ever bought or sold any of the wine to any man—had confessed on that day and place and still confessed that he had caused Laurence Boy and his companions to carry 9 pipes of the 15 tuns of John Brykles' wine out of the vessel of Brittany into the cellar of his place in the town of Fowey. Afterwards on 16 January 1432, there at his place, he had delivered 8 pipes of the wine out of his cellar to Lord Botreaux, who had been present himself, and he and his men, by Thomas's deliverance had carried it away.

Thomas held one pipe of the wine still in his cellar for his own use. This was true on his oath.

Editor's Note. Three commissions to make inquiries in Cornwall and Devon were issued on the complaints of John Brykles of London and John Themovy, merchant and master of the ship *St. Guillaume* of Brittany. The first two were dated 14 and 21 July 1432, but the earlier one, which refers to the long suit of the complainants, is probably in error for 1433, the third was in October of the latter year. All three related to the seizing of the ship and the disposal of the complainant's wine after these had been taken to Fowey and ordered the discovery of the culprits and the causing of restitution to be made by them, or their appearance before the king and council. The two in 1433 named Laurence Boy as master of the *Mawdeleyn* and as captor with others unidentified (*CPR 1429–36* pp. 219, 220, 348).

Petition 29a above probably began John Brykles ' long suit ' and resulted in the commissions and the inquiries in Fowey which are referred to in 29b. The latter petition was no doubt presented after John Bodyer had been brought into court by the commission of October 1433, with the intention of obtaining redress from him for part of the wine which the inquiries had found to be in his possession.

Thomas Treffrye had been one of the eight commissioners appointed in July 1433 and was employed by the crown a few years later to arrest ships and as collector of customs in Plymouth and Fowey. (Ibid. p. 534, *CPR 1436–41* pp. 247, 313, 411).

30

CI/11/40 *French, some words illegible*

CHANCELLOR The bishop of Bath

DATE 4 March 1432–1435

PETITIONER Massior Lestuvel, attorney in this suit[1] for the merchants of Rouen.

COMPLAINT Various goods and merchandise had been forcibly taken[2] by a number of wrongdoers of Devonshire and Cornwall, of whom one, called Laurence Bouy, a German,[3] had seized a ship of Rouen called *Saint Eustace*, owned by Pieriee Preere of Rouen. The inquiry held at Exeter by John Upton and Edward Pomeroy had disclosed that Laurence Bouy was the master of a balinger owned by William [Chattoy][4] of Plymouth, and the finding of an inquiry taken at Plymouth by James Chiddley, John Jaybyn, and William Pollard of Plymouth, commissioners on behalf of a Breton named John Themovy had also made it known to the chancellor.

REQUEST That because of this the chancellor would recall[5] [the wrongdoers and administer to the king's subjects] true justice in the sight of God, and the king their sovereign lord would be greatly obliged to him on behalf of his true and loyal subjects, and the petitioner would pray to God for him.[6]

[1] *en ceste partie*
[2] *pressa prisee*
[3] *almand*; cp. 29b above: Laurence Boy, *doucheman*.
[4] *Katoith*
[5] *reviendrer*
[6] The writing is partly illegible, but this seems to be the sense of the passage. Normandy was under English rule and Henry VI had been formally crowned king of France in December 1431.

Editor's Note. No entries have been found on the patent rolls in which either John Upton and Edward Pomeroy, who was sheriff of Devon, or

James Chiddley, sheriff of Cornwall, John Jaybyn and William Pollard were on commissions together, but one or other of them were among the men ordered to make inquiries into complaints by Pieriee Preere and other burgesses of Rouen in 1431 and 1432 as well as that of John Themovy and John Brykeles. Pieriee Preere and the others of Rouen were suing for recovery of ships of Rouen and Brittany seized by west country men contrary ' to the final peace concluded between the king's realms of France and England'. He and burgesses of the king's cities of Paris and Rouen were seeking redress for the carrying off ' as though they belonged to the enemy,' of other ships in 1434 and 1435 (*CPR 1429–36* pp. 127, 128, 201, 219, 356, 525). Laurence Boy was not named among the offenders in either case.

31

C1/10/21 *French*

CHANCELLOR The bishop of Bath

DATE 4 March 1432–February 1433

PETITIONER Ralph Trevysa of Plymouth in the county of Devonshire, merchant.

COMPLAINT Thomas Lacom of Plymouth had arrested without cause 300 stakes,[1] a silver mounted hamper and 100 lbs[2] of wool belonging to the petitioner, valued at £7 in a ship on the sea, and still kept them under arrest to the petitioner's great damage unless he had the chancellor's aid and succour.

REQUEST That the chancellor would grant a writ directed to Thomas Lacom to appear before him in the king's chancery on a certain day and penalty fixed by him to answer in the matter for God etc. and in consideration of the petitioner's lack of remedy at common law because Thomas Lacom was water bailiff at Plymouth and would not obey a king's writ or any other warrant of the sheriff for anything done or arrested in the water of Plymouth.

[1] iii^c *de pesson'*
[2] c *lb'*

Editor's Note. Thomas Lacom was on commissions in 1432 and 1433; another man seems to have been water bailiff in Plymouth from February 1433 (*CPR 1429–36* pp. 219, 300, 301. Ibid. *1435–41* p. 432). The office included authority to hold a court in the king's name and to take all the fees and profits arising from it. It was usual to grant it as a reward for good service. (*CPR 1436–41* p. 229).

32

C1/10/37

CHANCELLOR The bishop of Bath

DATE May 1432–July 1433

PETITIONER Clays Classon, master and owner of the *Katherine of Dunkirk* in Flanders.

COMPLAINT The petitioner and his ship had recently, on 22 May, been seized at sea on the Trade[1] of St. Mathieu in Brittany by Englishmen of London and Dartmouth. After taking the ship they brought it to Dartmouth, and there the baron of Carew and a certain Gille[2] had taken possession of it and would not release it because they said that the goods in it belonged to French men. The petitioner knew that this was not so and said that the goods belonged to James de Clerk, John Launser of Bruges, and John Gaunsecutes all three merchants of Sluis in Flanders. James de Clerk had a hundred salt for brewage[3] and 22 tuns of wine in the ship, John Launser and John Gaunsecutes had a hundred salt each, and the petitioner had a hundred salt. He would swear before the chancellor upon the book that these goods did not belong to French men but to the above named merchants and he would prove it to be true. Also William Vandirdern of Bruges and Adrian Laman, merchant of Damme in Flanders, had 11 tuns and a pipe of wine and 14 tuns and a pipe of wine respectively in the ship, which the petitioner knew well was Flemish, but he would not swear it because French men had delivered it and laid it in the ship. The petitioner was at great loss and hindrance from the taking and retaining of the ship and goods which was causing him great distress.[4]

REQUEST That the chancellor would grant him delivery of his ship and goods, or his own goods and those of the three merchants for whom he would take oath if he might not have the goods of the other two, for the love of God etc.

[1] *Tarde*=trade or rade? i.e.: roadstead.
[2] Thomas Gille, cp. editor's note below and 39 p. 41
[3] *bruage*=a boiling (i.e. of salt); *the hundredth salt bruage, a measure of capacity.* O.E.D.
[4] *grete hevinesse and disease*

Editor's Note. On 8 July 1433, Robert Large, citizen and merchant of London entered into a recognizance for £100 to be paid to Thomas Gille and Thomas Broun if James le Clerk, merchant of Damme, and Clays Classon of Dunkirk, both places in Flanders, did not abide by and carry out the judgement of the bishop of Bath and Wells, chancellor, concerning 22 tuns of wine and 400 of salt of the measure of ' burwage ' in a ship called the *Katherine of Dunkirk*, of which Clays was master, taken on the high sea by men of Dartmouth; provided that the judgement was delivered by the next Easter (*CCR 1429–36* p. 259).
  Several years later Clays Classon was master of a Dutch ship loaded by London merchants which put into Kirkley Road near Yarmouth for fear of enemies. John Cornyssh, master of a balinger of Plymouth carrying

armed men, came to the same port and made friends with the merchants and pursuaded them that they could sail safely to London and when they did so he had attacked and carried off their ship (*CPR 1436–41* p. 506).

33

C1/11/204 *French, badly damaged*

CHANCELLOR The bishop of Bath

DATE July 1433–24 February 1434

PETITIONER John Chirche, citizen and mercer of London.

COMPLAINT On 21 July 1432 the king with the advice and assent of his council had granted to the petitioner, by letters patent under the great seal, licence [to go and/or send agents?] freely and peacefully to the kingdom of Spain to trade and return to England without hindrance as often as he wished during the next three years. Authorized by this licence, he had bought, by his agent Jonetto Salvayge, 8 tuns of oil in the town of Seville in Spain at £10 a tun. [The oil had been loaded in?] a caravel of Genoa for its safe carriage to the port of Sandwich in England to the use and profit of the petitioner, together with various other merchandise belonging to various Genoese and other persons. [While the caravel?] was at sea sailing towards England, John Myxstowe of Fowey, Thomas Adam and John Waterman, both of Polruan, John Porth of St. Austyn[1] with John Perkyn, William Phelyppe of [. . .] merchant, John and Martin Roch and John Evyll of Taunton and others unknown, amounting to 200 persons, had come on 26 July 1433 in a great ship called the *Edward* and a balinger, armed and arrayed for [war, and captured the Genoese caravel?] and brought it to Fowey and despoiled it there of all the goods and merchandise in it. Though the petitioner had given notice to the wrongdoers that the 8 tuns were his and required them to make [restitution?] never [theless] they were refusing to do so to his great damage and loss unless he had the chancellor's support and aid in the matter.

REQUEST That the chancellor would consider the foregoing and also that the tuns of oil were still [in the hands of the wrongdoers?] and grant several writs directing the aforesaid persons to appear before him in the king's chancery under a certain pain and on a day fixed by him; and if the abovesaid matter and complaint were found true by examination or in any other way, that then the petitioner should recover what he was claiming,[2] with the costs and damages suffered by him because of the capture, for God etc.

[1] St. Austell?
[2] *soit restorez a son demaunde*

Editor's Note. The merchants of Genoa among whose goods John Chirche's oil had been loaded were living in London, and they also brought a complaint into chancery about the capture by John Myxstowe, master of a ship of Fowey, and others—including four of those named by John Chirche—of their carrack, master: Luke de Matheo, and its cargo. According to their complaint the vessel had been on the high sea off cape St. Vincent, bound for Sandwich, when it was seized. The crew, it was alleged, had offered no resistance, nevertheless, they had been put ashore in a destitute state in Portugal, falsely accused of being Saracens. The ship had been taken to Fowey and the cargo divided among the captors and disposed of in the counties of Cornwall, Devon, Somerset and Wiltshire. The merchants had offered to prove their ownership before the mayor of Fowey and the captors in accordance with the statute (27 Edw. III stat. 2) but redress was being refused. Commissioners were appointed on 24 February 1434 to hold inquiries (*CPR 1429–36* p. 355). Another commission was enrolled on the same day giving instructions to four men to enquire who was then in possession of John Chirche's 8 tuns of oil and also of 5 tuns belonging to Walter Fetiplace of Southampton which had been plundered in the same carrack. This entry on the patent roll was, however, cancelled because nothing was done in the matter. The Genoese merchants obtained one more commission some six months later, ordering the arrest of the carrack and the goods taken out of it, and the appearance before the king and council of those who resisted (*CPR 1429–36* pp. 352, 469).

34

C1/69/366 *French, some words illegible*

CHANCELLOR To the very reverend father in God and very gracious lord the chancellor.

DATE Uncertain 1430–1440

PETITIONER Steven Hales of Southwark.

COMPLAINT Before the previous Michaelmas, the petitioner had loaded a ship of Clyve, of which Richard Hore of Clyve was master, with two long cloths, one black and the other [. . .], cocketed, as appeared on the London customs rolls. The cocket[1] had been delivered to one of the seamen of the ship, which had sailed before he returned and he was left behind and embarked in another ship.[2] When the ship of Clyve came to Plymouth, the searchers there found the cloths and because the cocket was missing they seized and detained them to the great damage and loss of the petitioner.

REQUEST That the chancellor for God and in work of charity would order a writ to the searchers of Plymouth to release the cloths seeing that the London customs officers would record that they had been properly cocketed.

French
Endorsed: The searchers of London were to be called and examined on this matter and the searchers of Plymouth instructed on it.

A second endorsement is nearly obliterated. It seems to be dated 25 December, year illegible, and to certify that the cloth had been customed.

¹A document delivered to merchants by the customs officers certifying that duty had been paid on their merchandise and the payment entered on the roll. *O.E.D.*
²*quant le dit nief segla avaunt il dev'ia derer' un marr' et passa en un autre nief*

Editor's Note. No indication of date has been found, nor has Clyve been identified. There are references to Cleves or Cliffe in Gelderland and Netherlanders were dwelling in Southwark in 1436 (*CPR 1429-36* p. 584, 541).

35

C1/69/122 *French, badly damaged*

CHANCELLOR The very noble and gracious lord the chancellor of England

DATE Uncertain 1430–40

PETITIONER Hugh Yon

COMPLAINT During the previous November, the petitioner had recovered [in the admiral's court from John ....?] and been put in possession of, three quarters of the ship called the *Marie of Dartmouth* of which the aforesaid John was owner, as appeared more plainly [in the record of the admiral's court?] Recently John Baron of Exeter maliciously and in maintenance of John [   ] had caused the petitioner to be arrested in the staple court in the city of Exeter and had him imprisoned there with the intention [that he should not?] recover the three quarters of the ship, contrary to all right and reason and in contempt of the admiral [and of his jurisdiction and to the damage?] of the petitioner unless he had a remedy from the chancellor.

REQUEST That the chancellor would consider the matter and, [in the interest of] the admiral and in support of the jurisdiction of his court, grant the petitioner a writ of *corpus cum causa* directed to the mayor and constables of the staple in Exeter to be returned on a given day when the matter could be [examined?] for God and charity.

Editor's Note. Hugh Yon was one of the eight men appointed to arrest and restore to Pieriee Preere and other burgesses of Rouen their ship and goods captured contrary to the peace between England and France in 1431. Later in the same year he was himself named among a long list of men accused of capturing Flemish goods and treating them as enemy property, also, it was alleged, at a time of peace (30 above, p. 33; *CPR 1429-36* pp. 127-8, 154). Ten years later he and eleven others were commissioned to receive from all masters of ships leaving Dartmouth bonds undertaking that they would not seize the goods of law abiding subjects of the Duke of Brittany with whom the king had recently concluded a treaty (*CPR 1441-46* p. 48). For other complaints against John Baron of Exeter during the same period see below 36, note p. 39.

36

C1/74/12

CHANCELLOR The right reverend gracious lord the chancellor

DATE 1436–37

PETITIONER William Tuke, mercer of Exeter.

COMPLAINT Nicholas, baron of Carreu, John Copleston, William Cok', John Hull, Roger Burgh and John Baron, merchant of Exeter, had been commissioned four years and more earlier to inquire into the seizing at sea by a number of the king's people of a vessel and certain goods owned by John Donnart and Merian Pascu, merchants of Brittany, contrary to the long standing truce between this land and Brittany. The inquiry held by virtue of the commission had found into whose hands the goods had come and restitution had been made, but John Baron had extortionately taken a pipe of the petitioner's bastard wine[1] claiming that the commission had empowered him so to do.[2] In the same way, upon pretext of the commission, he had taken and kept for his own use from every man in the neighbourhood towards whom he bore ill will, two packs of cloth from some, and one from some, so that no man dared to trade[3] without taking a tribute to him, whereby the king lost his customs and his people were greatly wronged.

REQUEST That the chancellor would consider the matter and grant a writ directed to John Baron ordering him under an adequate penalty to appear on a given day before the king and council to be examined concerning the matter for the love of God etc.

Pledges of prosecution: Henry Brok, Robert Carsewill

[1] A sweet Spanish wine.
[2] *beryng hym an honor (?) that he had power to make it be vertue of the foresaide comission*
[3] *soo that der noo man use ther noo merchandise*

Editor's Note. In addition to the commission referred to in this petition, which was dated 24 August 1432 (above, 28 p. 30), John Baron had been employed on others to inquire into complaints of unlawful seizure of ships and goods in 1432 and 1433 (*CPR 1429–36* pp. 202, 300). He was one of the defendants in an action of trespass in 1434, and in June 1435 the mayor and sheriff of Exeter were ordered to arrest him and the man who had lately been mayor and two other merchants of the same town: no reason was given. In October 1436, however, when he was one of many men of the west and south-west whose arrest was ordered, it was because they were all said to have taken part in carrying off a ship under letters of safe conduct from a Breton harbour. Just over six months later, ten men, including the mayors of Dartmouth and Exeter, were ordered to arrest him to answer unspecified charges in chancery brought against him by the king and Giles Haddon (Ibid. pp. 431 474, *1436–41* pp. 83, 87). Neither Hugh Yon (above, 35) nor William Tuke were named in any of these proceedings, but their petitions and the complaint of Donnart and Pascu (above, 28) probably indicate the kind of offences for which John Baron was being prosecuted.

37

C1/69/196 *French, damaged*

CHANCELLOR The very gracious lord the chancellor of England

DATE 1431–1441

PETITIONERS John le Pennick, Martyn Jahaiet, Morevard le Jontour of Guerande in Brittany.

COMPLAINT The petitioners, the true owners[1] of a barge called [. . .] of Guerande, had freighted it with various merchandise of their own i.e.: salt, iron, and linen cloth valued at £120, at Guerande. When coming with it and the cargo to the port of [. . .] in the county of Cornwall, they had been taken on the high sea by John Colvyle of Plymouth and other men unknown to them, arrayed for war, and imprisoned and despoiled of their barge and merchandise to their great damage[2] unless they had the chancellor's aid and support.

REQUEST That he would consider the matter and grant a writ addressed to John [Colvyle ordering him to appear in chancery] on a given day to be examined on the matter and to do what right and reason required, and they would pray to God for the chancellor.

[1] *loialment possessez de un lour barge*, i.e. they were not covering enemy property?
[2] *grant destruccion*

Editor's Note. This petition seems to belong to the same period as the previous three and the one following, in none of which is the chancellor identified. John Colvyle was named among a number of west-country men and others against whom complaints were made between 1431 and 1436 by merchants of Italy and Aragon in London, a seaman of Bayonne, and merchants of Flanders. In each case the claim was for goods seized at sea and wrongly treated as enemy property. In one of them John Colvyle was described as the master of a balinger of Plymouth, and in another John Rygelyn was one of the alleged culprits (*CPR 1429–36* pp. 199, 200, 352, 527). The two merchants of Plymouth named John Rigulyn and John Colville who, forty years or more earlier, had bought figs and raisins from Fernando Alfonso of Lisbon (above, 1 p. 1) were probably older members of the same families. In 1441 John Colvyle of Plymouth, seaman, was pardoned of outlawry for not appearing before the king to answer concerning certain trespasses with which he was charged. He had surrendered to the Marshalsea prison (*CPR 1436–41* p. 549). A John Pennok, merchant of Brittany, was trading in salt with Robert Russell of Bristol in 1413 (above, 16 p. 19).

38

Ci/73/161

CHANCELLOR The right reverend father in God and gracious lord the chancellor of England

DATE Probably 1436

PETITIONER Lambert Smyth, merchant of the Hanse and servant to the duke of Guelders.[1]

COMPLAINT In the previous January, the petitioner had bought 26 tuns of white wine of la Rochelle, 14 tuns of which had been loaded in a hulk of Sluis, master: John Groull, and 12 tuns in a barge also of Sluis, Hayne Huvee, master, the price of the whole 26 tuns amounting to £120. In April, Thomas Gylle of Kingsbridge, owner of the *Anthony of Dartmouth*, John White, master, had seized the hulk and barge on the coast of Normandy with the wine. He had carried off the wine to England. Some of it bearing the petitioner's mark, had found been in the possession of John Sturgeon, mercer of London.

REQUEST That the chancellor would grant a writ *subpoena* directed to Thomas Gylle ordering him to appear in chancery under a fixed penalty and on a given day, so that the petitioner might recover his wine or its value as good faith and conscience required, at reverence of God and for charity.

[1]*Gylder*

Editor's Note. Thomas Gylle had received a licence in February 1436 to send the *Anthony of Dartmouth* to sea against the enemy. John Sturgeon was similarly licensed for a ship of London in the following September (below 39, note p. 42 and *CPR 1436–41* p. 1).

39

Ci/11/245 *French*

CHANCELLOR The bishop of Bath

DATE 1437

PETITIONER Thomas Gille

COMPLAINT Nicholas Hawley of Dartmouth, esquire, and Thomas Loveney of Norton[1] in the county of Devonshire, gentleman, had been arrested recently in Exeter by the justices of the peace, at the request of the petitioner, to find security to keep the peace towards himself and all other subjects of the king, and had been bound over[2] by the justices until the next session of the peace after the following Christmas. But in this Michaelmas term 1437, Nicholas and Thomas Loveney had come into chancery, with four other unknown men who had neither land nor rents, and undertaken falsely in small sums to keep the peace towards someone other than the petitioner, with the intention of taking vengeance upon him and his servants and also to prevent the construction of a great ship which the petitioner was building in Dartmouth.

REQUEST That the chancellor would consider that Nicholas was worth[3] 300 marks of land and rent and Thomas Loveney £10 of annual rent and also how they had deceived the king in this case and grant a writ of attachment to the sheriff of Devonshire, with an adequate penalty, for their arrest to answer the king in chancery for their deceit. For God etc.

[1] *Nordon*
[2] *miz en baille*
[3] *est homme sufficeaunt de*

Editor's Note. Thomas Gille or Gylle of Kingsbridge and Dartmouth was a shipowner of some substance in the third and fourth decades of the century. He was one of a number of men—the others all of London and north-eastern ports—who were licensed in 1436 to equip ships at their own expense with masters and seamen, men-at-arms, archers and other habiliments of war and victuals to resist the king's enemies at sea for four months. His licences were for the *Anthony of Dartmouth* (John White, master), and the *Katherine* (John Lesard, master), with two balingers or barges; they gave express permission for captured vessels and goods to belong to the captors, saving to the admiral of England and the warden of the Cinque ports their customary shares; and they contained a proviso that the owner and victuallers of a captor ship were not to be held responsible for offences against the king's friends: only those who committed them would be answerable (*CPR 1429–36* p. 509; Ibid. *1436–41* p. 1).

He was frequently called upon between 1431 and 1435 with others to hold inquiries and arrest men, ships or goods in the west country as a result of complaints about unlawful captures. He was also commissioned to arrest ships in Exeter for the passage of the duke of York to France (*CPR 1429–36* pp. 132, 201, 220, 301, 525). In 1439 he was one of the collectors of customs in Exeter and Dartmouth (Ibid. p. 247). The complaints made against him in earlier petitions no doubt arose out of the disputes which must inevitably have occurred in the carrying out of his official duties (above 32 and 38 below 45 and notes pp. 35, 41, 47).

Nicholas Hawley, the son of John Hawley the younger, who had died in May 1436, was about 22 years old at this time (Watkin 1935 pp. 414–15).

40

C1/9/171 *French, many words illegible*

CHANCELLOR The bishop of Bath

DATE 20 February–14 May 1438

PETITIONER James Lamme, called in his own language Copin Lamme, merchant of Middleburg.

COMPLAINT On 16 February 1438, Edward Hampton, otherwise called Edward Jolyff of [Topsham] near Exeter, merchant, caused William Bele of Exminster to arrest 7 bales of madder and 2 bales of alum, price £36, of the petitioner's goods in Topsham. On the following 20 February, the said Edward arrested 5 sacks of hops, price 20 marks [of the petitioner's] goods in Dartmouth, alleging[1] that they belonged to Thomas Jacobysson of Middleburg, whereas, in truth and faith, all the aforesaid goods which came out of Middleburg before the [feast of St.] John belonged to the petitioner and not to Thomas Jacobysson. To obtain deliverance of them, the petitioner had offered to prove by sufficient proofs before [William Bele(?) according to the] use and custom of Topsham that the 7 bales of madder and 2 bales of alum were his own goods without fraud or deceit,[2] [and that the 5 sacks of hops were also his(?)] and not the goods of Thomas Jacobysson.

Notwithstanding all aforesaid, Edward Jolyff and William Bele were still keeping the 7 bales of madder and 2 bales of alum [and the 5 sacks of hops] to the complete hindrance and ruin of the petitioner unless he had the chancellor's aid.

REQUEST That the chancellor of his special grace would consider the matter and [issue writs] directed to Edward Jolyff and William Bele to appear before the king in chancery on a certain day and under a penalty to be fixed by the chancellor, to be examined concerning [the matter and to do what right] and conscience require, for God's love etc.

Latin Memorandum: That on 14 May 1438 John Payn of Southampton in the county of Southampton, husbandman, and Alexander Reve of London, merchant, mainperned for the petitioner before the king in chancery [that] should he be unable to prove the matter specified in this petition to be true, then he would satisfy John Payn for all the damages and expenses sustained by Edward Jolyff and William Bele on this account, in accordance with the form of the statute provided for this case.[3]

[1] *surmittyng*
[2] *male engyn'*
[3] See Introduction p. xviii

Editor's Note. No record of any other proceedings concerning this complaint has been found. In 1441, however, ' Copyn Lamb ' and another merchant of Middleburg together with the captain and master, three named seamen and other unknown men, all of Zeeland and Holland, were found by an inquiry to have made an armed attack near Southampton on the ship of a man of Cadiz in Spain. They were accused of capturing it when it was coming to England under letters of safe conduct. The keeper of the privy seal, a doctor of laws and four others were commissioned to try the charge (*CPR 1436–41* p. 575).

41

C1/43/35

CHANCELLOR The bishop of Bath

DATE 1438–13 May 1443

PETITIONER John, Lord Talbot and Furnyvale

COMPLAINT In December 1438, the petitioner's ship the *Margaret of Portla-down*, valued at 100 marks, was on the high sea sailing to the port of Rouen[1] carrying 369 quarters of salt, valued at 13s. 4d. a quarter, which were seized and shared out by a number of rioters and wrongdoers unknown to the petitioner in a balinger, the *Jenot of Fowey*, of which Thomas Jerard of Fowey was part owner. He had condoned the capture and taken his share, to the great hindrance of the petitioner without a remedy from the chancellor.

REQUEST That the chancellor would consider the foregoing and grant a writ directed to Thomas Jerard to appear before him on a day and under a penalty given by him to be examined concerning the matter, and to be ruled at his discretion, for the love of God etc.

[1]*Roone*

42

C1/45/130

CHANCELLOR The bishop of Bath

DATE June 1439–13 May 1443

PETITIONER William Halle

COMPLAINT The petitioner's ship, *Markys de London*, loaded with salt for London, had been taken at sea on the west coast by robbers threatening armed attack[1] in June 1439. John Werde of Plympton had carried away out of it 40 quarters of the petitioner's salt, each quarter containing 11 [. . .][2] and priced at 22s., as the share due to the lord of Devonshire for a ship, the *Moton*, which was one of the captors of the *Markys*. John Werde was withholding the goods, to the petitioner's great damage without the chancellor's aid in obtaining their recovery.

REQUEST That he would consider the foregoing and grant a writ directed to John Werde to appear in chancery upon a day and under a penalty to be fixed by the chancellor to be examined in the matter in the honour of God etc.

[1]*be extorcion with force and arms*
[2]an undecipherable abbreviation; perhaps bushels?

43

C1/43/13 *Some words illegible*

CHANCELLOR The bishop of Bath

DATE October 1439–13 May 1443

PETITIONERS Richard Perowe, Baldwin Henry, John Povna, Henry Aunger, Peter Jonherry, Michael Robert, John Herry and John Richowe, the poor fishermen of the port of St. Ives, Cornwall.[1]

COMPLAINT On the Monday after the previous mid-Lent Sunday, Hugh Wytford, lately mayor of Bristol, had made his servant, John William, merchant of the same town, sue and affirm a plaint of trespass against the petitioners in the court in Bristol, over which Hugh Wytford had jurisdiction and power,[2] alleging that trespass by taking of goods and chattels had been committed by the arrest of certain of Hugh's goods and chattels when they were in John William's keeping in Cornwall. The petitioners had not been in any way connected with or consenting to the arrest, nor had been guilty of any trespass against Hugh Wytford or John William in Cornwall or anywhere else, as they were ready to prove in whatever way the chancellor would award.[3] Yet by virtue of the abovesaid plaint, 1 cwt. barrel of grease,[4] priced at £100, of their goods had been arrested in a ship lying in the port of Bristol; and later because of the same plaint, the petitioners themselves had been arrested and imprisoned in irons and detained, until John William had received judgement to recover his goods and had execution of the barrel of grease i.e. of £100, which John had paid to Thomas Marke by order of Hugh Wytford to whose use it had come.

Afterwards since the value of the cwt. barrel of grease did not come to the whole sum which Hugh Wytford and John William were supposed to have recovered, Hugh caused the keeper of the prison in which the petitioners were to bring them to his house, where he fixed on each of them a certain sum in excess of the value of the said cwt. barrel; and because they had not sufficient goods or money to satisfy him, they found a guarantor[5] in Bristol, i.e. the aforesaid Thomas Merke, merchant of Bristol, who had satisfied Hugh Wytford of all that he demanded. Nevertheless the petitioners had been kept in prison for another 7 days, to their utter ruin unless they had the chancellor's aid and support.

REQUEST That the chancellor would consider the foregoing and grant writs directed to Hugh Wytford and John William to appear in the king's chancery on a certain day under a certain penalty fixed by him to be examined on all the circumstances and to be judged, so that the petitioners should have due remedy in accordance with right and conscience for the love of God etc.

Pledges of prosecution: William Hay, Ralph Trewyk

[1] *the pouer Fysshers of the Port of Seint Tya in the Shire of Cornwayll*
[2] *where the said Hugh had reule and governance*
[3] *they been redy to averre and make it good as ye will awarde*
[4] *an a. barrell of seyme i.e. 1 cwt. of seam grease. O.E.D.*
[5] *a borowe*

Editor's Note. Hugh Wytford was mayor of Bristol during the year beginning Michaelmas 1438 (*CPR 1436–41* p. 268).

44

C1/43/20 *Some words illegible*

CHANCELLOR The bishop of Bath

DATE 23 May 1433–1443

PETITIONER Lambert Whitynburgh of Danzig in Prussia.

COMPLAINT On the previous 15 January, the petitioner was master of a ship, the *Isabell of Danzig*, loaded with Flemish merchandise, lying in the port of Plymouth, when Robert Wodmanston, captain of a balinger called the *Mighel of Bordeaux* (John Elys master), and many others of their confederacy[1] in it had come and entered the *Isabell* with force and arms and took possession of it and all its tackle and plundered it of clothing, armour and chests of the petitioner and his seamen. The value of the ship's tackle was £90 and that of the clothing, armour and chests £17 13s. 4d., and the loss of the freight for the cargo, £100, amounting in all to £207 13s. 4d. On the following 10 March, Thomas Carmynow, esquire, at the instigation of Master John Waryn and Robert Wodmanston, arrested the ship and tackle and kept it under arrest, so that it was lost to the petitioner. Later, on the 23 March, Thomas Carmynow's servant, Robert Pale, arrested the petitioner and kept him under arrest till he had paid a fine and ransom [against his will and to his?] harm and damages in addition to the principal sum of £100.

REQUEST That the chancellor would consider his complaint and call before him Thomas Carmynow, [Robert Wodman]ston and Robert Pale, who were then present in the court[2] to be examined in the matter and the circumstances, and ordain due remedy so that the petitioner had no cause to complain in any other [court for the love] of God etc.

[1] *of her covyn'*
[2] *being here present*

Editor's Note. Thomas Carymnow served on various commissions in the west of England in 1434 and 1435 (*CPR 1429–36* pp. 469, 474, 475, 519). It is possible that his part in the offence complained of above followed a commission in which he was not mentioned, dated according to the patent roll, 20 February 1440 and issued to the sheriff of Devon and six other men to hold an inquiry concerning an information made on behalf of Lambert Whitynburgh. The latter was described as master of the *Isabell of Danzig* and also as part owner of it; four merchants of Flanders were named who, with the others of king's friendship, had cargo in the ship. It had been lying peacefully in Plymouth harbour when Robert Wodmanston, lately of London, gentleman, who called himself the captain of a balinger of war, the *Michael of Bordeaux*, and other wrongdoers had attacked and boarded the *Isabell*, driven Whitynburgh and the merchants out of it, imprisoned the crew under hatches and seized and carried off goods of theirs contrary to the truce between the king and the Flemings. Those found guilty were to be imprisoned till further order and restitution was to be made of the goods or their value (*CPR 1436–41* p. 409).

45a

C1/43/33 *Damaged*

CHANCELLOR The bishop of Bath

DATE 1440

PETITIONER William Waleys, born at Lancaster, England, dwelling at Drogheda in Ireland, merchant.

COMPLAINT On 21 January 1440, the petitioner had been in a ship called the *George of Welles*, of 120 tons, with goods valued at £600, at Start Point,[1] 7 miles from the port of Dartmouth in Devonshire. At the time a ship called the *Christopher of Dartmouth*, 320 tons, of which Thomas Gyll was then the owner and victualler[2] and Richard Walter master, had been ahead of the *George*, inside Start Point nearer Dartmouth, where it might have stayed in shelter as other ships (which had come with it[3]) did. But Richard Walter, seeing the *George* coming behind him 3 miles away, turned the *Christopher* round, and with full sail and a favourable wind[4] and 3 well harnessed men in the topcastle and others, to the number of 40, arrayed for war distributed about it, that ship struck away the foreship of the *George* so that it and all the goods and merchandise in it were lost and sunk. But for the grace of God, the petitioner and everyone else, numbering about 44 persons, would have perished also, although he had called out to Richard Walter that they were Englishmen and had their sails set back and their hull lying low.[5]

REQUEST That the chancellor would consider the foregoing and examine Thomas Gyll, who was present in the court, concerning it and, if he were found guilty by examination or in any other way cause him to make restitution to the petitioner for his goods and losses in the case. He also prayed consideration for his great poverty, loss and delays, and for being from a distant country and ignorant about Dartmouth, whereas Thomas Gyll lived there and was well known in the town, and had great authority and power in the district.[6]

[1] *The Sterte*
[2] *yhittes'*
[3] *that com wyth hym*, reading found in 45c only
[4] *a large wynde*
[5] *lay upon the lee wyth ther corse low sett*, indicating that they were coming into port, not in fighting trim or trying to escape.
[6] Cp. above 39, note p. 42

45b

C1/44/278

CHANCELLOR The bishop of Bath

DATE 1440

PETITIONER Robert Langherste, born at Newcastle-upon-Tyne, dwelling at Drogheda in Ireland, merchant.

COMPLAINT Identical with 45a

REQUEST Identical with 45a.

45c

C1/45/141 *Damaged*

CHANCELLOR The bishop of Bath

DATE 1440, after 12 June

PETITIONER Robert Langherste, born at Newcastle-upon-Tyne etc. (as in 45b).

COMPLAINT On the Tuesday after the conversion of St. Paul[1] 1440, the petitioner had been in a ship, etc. (as in 45a)

REQUEST Identical with 45a down to the end i.e. Thomas Gyll . . . had great authority and power in the district. Then follows a statement that since the alleged offences had been fully proved before the chancellor in the king's chancery by sufficient proofs and witnesses, as the record showed, the king had recently sent a commission to Master John Stokkes to examine the truth of the matter, which he had done; and the commission and examination had been returned and certified before the king in chancery where it remained on record. The petitioner prayed the chancellor to inspect the examination and, having done so, to grant him satisfaction for the offence in accordance with his wisdom as right and reason required, for the love of God etc.

[1]25 January.

45d

C1/10/30 *Badly damaged*

CHANCELLOR The bishop of Bath

DATE 1440, after 12 June

PETITIONER William Walys, born in Lancaster, etc. (as in 45a)

COMPLAINT The document is so mutilated that it is impossible to recon-
struct the contents, but there is little doubt that it is substantially the same
as 45C and that the request includes the reference to the commission to
Master John Stokkes.

Editor's Note The commission referred to in these petitions was addressed
to the king's clerk, master John Stokes, doctor of laws, and entered on the
patent roll on 12 June 1440. It authorised him to hear a maritime action
pending in chancery between the two petitioners of Drogheda and Thomas
Gyll of Dartmouth, to call and examine witnesses and any others
necessary to ascertain the truth, certifying the king of what he had done
(*CPR 1436–41* p. 451).

On 1 December 1440, reciprocal recognizances were recorded on the
close roll, binding Thomas Gyll on the one hand and William Walys,
Robert Langherst and Thomas Horwode on the other to abide by the
award of arbitrators—three named on Gyll's behalf and three on behalf
of the others—concerning all actions between the parties, provided that
the award was made before the following 10 February (*CCR 1435–41*
p. 445. Cp. 32 and 39 above, notes pp. 35, 42).

46a

C1/71/54

CHANCELLOR The chancellor of England

DATE 1440–1441

PETITIONERS John Fouler, Richard Boll with their company, merchants of
Drogheda in Ireland.

COMPLAINT The petitioners, loyal subjects of the king,[1] had loaded a ship
of Flanders, the *Christopher of Sluis*, with hides and horses from the port of
Drogheda to take to Port Sall[2] in Brittany and to reload with salt to bring
back to Ireland. But great gales and contrary weather had forced them
to take refuge in the port of Dartmouth, and there Robert Stephens,
bailiff of the town, took upon himself without writ or warrant or reasonable
cause to unload 34 horses, the goods and chattels of the petitioners. By so
doing he, together with Thomas Wise, esquire, had despoiled them of their
goods.

REQUEST That the chancellor would send for Robert Stephens, by a writ
under a penalty fixed by him, summoning Stephens to appear before the
king, his judges and ministers in chancery wherever it was on the quindene
of Hilary, to hear and abide by and submit to such things as would be
declared against him by the petitioners and their counsel, for the love of
God etc.

[1]*the kingis triew liege poeple*
[2]*Salus*

46b

Cı/45/25

CHANCELLOR The bishop of Bath and Wells

DATE 1440–1

PETITIONERS The king's loyal subjects,[1] merchants of Ireland.

COMPLAINT The petitioners had loaded a ship of Flanders, the *Christopher of Sluis* (John Groitom master and owner), with hides and 34 horses, intending to take them to Port Sall[2] in Brittany and to reload the ship with salt and return to Ireland with it to provision that country. It happened that—to save themselves, their merchandise and the ship in a great gale—the petitioners had entered the port of Dartmouth, where Thomas Wise of Devonshire, esquire, had removed and concealed the 34 horses alleging that they were forfeit, which they were not, as the petitioners were ready to prove there and then by their charter party and cockets sealed in Ireland, which recorded the destination and purpose of the voyage and also that the custom, subsidy and duty had been duly paid.

REQUEST That the chancellor, of his conscience and since he was an authority on the law, would urge the king to ordain and pronounce a remedy which would enable them to recover their own property speedily and not be plundered of it in this noble realm, taking into consideration that horses were a most important part of Ireland's trade. Or else that he would give them whatever answer he thought lawful so that they should not be ruined, for God's love and charity.

[1] *the kyng our soverain lordes triew lieges*
[2] *to make theire port Saluz*

Editor's Note. According to an entry on the patent roll, dated 11 December 1440, Thomas Wyse, king's esquire, had informed the king that a ship loaded in Ireland with horses for Brittany, without the king's licence, had been driven by storms on to the Devon coast where it and the horses had been confiscated for the crown. Assuming this to be true, the king had granted the horses to Wyse as a free gift, but reserving six of the best for himself (*CPR 1436–41* p. 484).

Thomas Wyse was a justice of the peace in Devon from 1439 and escheator, and was employed from time to time as a commissioner in the county. The only further reference to the complaint about the Irish horses is ambiguous. It is a memorandum on the close roll for 1446 of a general release to him of all personal actions by William Galway of Drogheda, merchant, attorney of the Irish merchants, to sue against him for horses he had taken in Dartmouth (*CPR 1436–41* pp. 274, 450. Ibid. *1441–46* p. 469, *CCR 1441–47* pp. 166, 438).

47

C1/75/96 *Many words illegible*

CHANCELLOR The chancellor

DATE 1440–3

PETITIONERS Laurence Wastell and John Ketynge, prisoners.

COMPLAINT On 2 July 1440, while at their occupation of fishing on the coasts of Dartmouth in 4 boats, i.e. 2 of D[artmouth? . . .] and the 4th of Teignmouth, the petitioners with others of their company had been taken to Dawet[1] in Brittany by John Gledou' of Dawet, and from there to Dinard in Brittany where the 4 boats had been ransomed for £46 16s. 8d. [. . . and having been?] thus ransomed they were bought out[2] by Nicholas Guille and Denis Philip, merchants of Guernsey, and they and others of their company entered into an obligation to Nicholas and Denis, for themselves and their company for the sum of £46 16s. [8d. . . . The petitioners and the others seem to have been released, leaving one of their number,] Roger Everard of Teignmouth, as hostage with the merchants of Guernsey until repayment of the amount of the ransom. But Wilberton [*sic*], a merchant of Kingsbridge in Devonshire, was withholding a great part of the ransom and [names? . . .] seamen, and the executors of William Perre of Teignmouth, John Knight, John Walssh,[3] William Geynecote and Richard Pauston of Dartmouth were withholding another large part of the same ransom: and a certain John Geynecote of Dartmouth [names of others?] who supported[4] the withholding of the ransom were all causing delay and preventing the ransom from being paid. Consequently the petitioners had been detained longer in prison and Roger Everard [. . . Laurence Wastell had taken the place of Roger Everard who, as a result of the delay caused by the above named and their?] supporters, had died in prison. The above named John Geyncote, with others of his following[5] had ambushed the petitioner, John Ketynge, with poleaxes and spears intending to kill him for asking for the ransom. Meanwhile the other petitioner, Laurence Wastell, [. . . whose place in prison had been taken by John Ketynge? . . .] And later when Laurence had come out of prison from Guernsey, and asked John Walssh for the ransom which he was withholding, the latter had assaulted him several times with drawn dagger in order [. . . to prevent him from pressing for payment of his contribution, and John Walssh was very powerful with his?] supporters, while the petitioners had been so hindered and made so poor by their pursuit of the ransom that they would be ruined for ever without the chancellor's aid.

REQUEST That he would consider this and issue[6] writs to the above named withholders of the ransom [. . . under] a penalty to those who were sufficient, and to order the baron of Carew and the mayor and bailiffs of Dartmouth to arrest the others to find sureties to answer in chancery on a given [day . . . what] should be declared against them. And also to send writs directing the baron and the mayor and bailiffs to arrest John Geynecote, John Walssh, William Geynecote, Walter Geynecote and Richard

Pauston to find sufficient [surety to appear and answer such charges] as should be made against them in due form, for the love of God etc.

¹Douarnenez?
²*bouzt out*
³Cp. 49 below
⁴*mayntenours of withholding* etc.
⁵*assunte*
⁶*sende out*

48a

C1/12/208

CHANCELLOR The bishop of Bath

DATE May 1441–October 1441

PETITIONERS Morvan Petyt and Piers Jary, merchants of Brittany.

COMPLAINT On the previous 31 May, the petitioners had been sailing with a ship called the *Christopher of St. Servan*, loaded with their goods, i.e. 35 tuns of wine of La Rochelle, with 4 more ships of their company of Brittany loaded with salt of the Bay, on their way to England to trade there, trusting in the peace lately made between the king of England and his uncle the duke of Brittany. But Haukyn Hoode, the master of a balinger of war of Falmouth, county Cornwall, and Simon Curteys, master of another balinger of war of the same place had come upon the five Breton ships on the sea near the Isle of Wight and seized them by force. They had returned one of them after plundering it of all its tackle and its boat, and taken the other four to Newport on the Isle of Wight. The petitioners' 35 tuns of wine were in one of these ships, and 150 weys of salt in the other three, the total value of the goods and merchandise being 500 marks sterling. The captors had sold a large quantity of them to Robert Aston, agent and attorney of John White of Newport; that is to say, Robert Aston had bought 35 tuns of Rochelle wine in the *St. Christopher* for and on behalf of John White from Haukyn Hood and his confederates for 40s. a tun.

The petitioners had complained concerning their 35 tuns, whereupon Robert Aston had entered the ship and disposed of 8 tuns as he wished. Then other men of the Isle of Wight, seeing such good wine being sold so cheap, came and said that they would take part of it after Robert had completed his deal; and then the steward of the island, William Leyot, came and decided how much each man should have—some being allotted a tun each and others more or less according to their friendship with him. Robert Aston had been a party to all this and to the delivery of the wine, and because he had previously bought the ship with the wine in gross, no man had dared to buy it.¹

REQUEST That the chancellor—as an example to others—would charge Robert Aston and John White and compel them to pay for the whole of the 35 tuns of wine at its value when captured, i.e. 5 marks a tun: total £116 13s. 4d. Also John Rove, William Barbour and John White and

Robert Aston of Newport with others of the same town, had taken into their keeping one of the petitioners' ships called a crayer, of 55 tons, with all its tackle saying that it had been given to them by Haukyn Hood and his confederates and therefore they intended to keep it, to the great prejudice of the petitioners and contrary to the peace treaty. The petitioners prayed therefore that John Rove and the others should be compelled to return the ship and 2 boats in as good condition as they had received them or pay what their value had been on the day of capture i.e.: £50 sterling, since they had been part of the ships taken by Haukyn and his confederates. The petitioners also prayed the chancellor to summon John Rove, William Barbour, John White and Robert Ashton and charge them on the book to say what had become of the rest of the aforesaid goods, since they knew where they were. This to be done for the love of God etc.

[1] *for aforetyme that he hadd bought the seyd shippe with wyn agret ther durst no man beye none thereof*

48b

C1/11/431 *Many words illegible. Referred to by C. L. Kingsford, 1925, pp. 90 ff.*

CHANCELLOR The bishop of Bath

DATE 29 June–26 October 1441

PETITIONERS Morvan Petyt and Piers Jary, merchants of Brittany.

COMPLAINT The petitioners had long been suing to the chancellor for restitution of several ships and their merchandise, i.e. wine and salt, which had been seized on the sea near the Isle of Wight on the previous 31 May by Haukyn Hoode and Simon Curteys living at Falmouth in county Cornwall, and brought to Newport in the Isle of Wight. There a ship called the *Christopher* and 35 tuns of wine belonging to the petitioners had been sold by Haukyn and his confederates to Robert Aston, proctor and attorney of John White of Newport.

Robert Aston and John White had recently appeared before the chancellor and the clerk of the [rolls?] and pleaded[1] that the goods had been taken by Hollanders and Zeelanders lawfully as they were enemies of the petitioners and their country, and also that the ship *Christopher* [. . . and the wine?] had belonged to the captain of Dieppe. But the petitioners could bring sufficient record that the said [wine was their own?] goods and marked with their marks, i.e. 20 tuns with one mark and 15 tuns with another, which marks they had ready to be [shown in court? Robert Aston and?] John White had affirmed also that they had only 4 pipes of the wine whereas the petitioners had alleged in their bill, put previously to the chancellor, that they had been in possession of the whole [35 tuns?] and had been dispossessed of it by William Leyot, steward of the Isle of Wight, according to whose ruling it had been apportioned and [as had been] confessed to Richard Clyfden, yeoman of the crown[1] and others. Robert Aston and his confederates had also affirmed that Haukyn Hood had given them and their parish a crayer of 15 tuns, and that they ought not to answer for it without the whole parish, which would cause the petitioners great delay. [. . .] sixteen writs *subpoena* had been direc- ted to the men of the Isle of Wight, but only four of them had appeared although the day given, i.e. the previous octave of Michaelmas, had passed.

REQUEST That the chancellor would consider the foregoing and the peace between England and Brittany, and that the clerk of the rolls had given Robert Aston and his confederates leave to go home and that [if they did] go their way it would be a great delay and most unjust obstruction of the petitioners who were too poor to remain and continue their suit, but must go home and lose their goods for lack of law, which would be contrary to all conscience; and that therefore Robert Aston and his confederates should stay in chancery and not find an attorney, and the petitioners should produce proof that the said good were their own, [and that Robert Aston and] his confederates were in possession of them, so that restitution of the ship and goods and the crayer might be made to the petitioners, for the [love of God etc.]

[1]Cp. 52 below p. 58

Editor's Note. Piers Jary joined with another Breton merchant, Elias de Gentill, and the master of the *Christopher of St. Servan* in a further complaint to the chancery court recorded in a commission entered on the patent roll on 29 June 1441, which gave the particulars set out in the two petitions above concerning the capture of this ship and the 4 others. An inquiry was to be held by six men including the sheriff of Southampton and William Leyot, whose alleged part in the subsequent sale of the wine was not mentioned. (*CPR 1436–41* p. 574). The appearance in court of Robert Aston and John White, referred to in 48b most probably followed this inquiry and led to an undertaking, recorded on 26 October 1441, by Robert Aston of Newport, kerseyman, and a William Oldebury of the town of Westminster, to pay £20 if Robert did not obey the award of the court of chancery concerning all contained in the petition presented against him and others named in it by Morvan Petyt and Piers Jary (*CCR 1441–7* p. 40).

49

C1/73/84

CHANCELLOR The chancellor of England

DATE 1442

PETITIONERS Thomas Roche of Taunton, John Chocherd and John Jemet, merchants of Dinan[1] in Brittany.

COMPLAINT On the Sunday before the previous feast of St. Thomas,[2] John Walssh of Dartmouth, seaman, and others of his confederacy had seized a pinnace belonging to John Chocherd and John Jemet in the harbour of

Brixham in Devonshire loaded with canvas, Dyneham cloth and iron of the petitioners valued at nearly £100. They had sued John Walssh for restitution of the goods and merchandise in accordance with the truce between the king and the duke of Brittany; but he would not return either the pinnace or their part of the goods and merchandise to John Chocherd and John Jemet, but had imprisoned them until they had made him a general acquittance. He had promised to return Thomas Roche's part of the goods and merchandise to him if he would make a general acquittance, which he had agreed to do; but after he had made it, John Walssh had refused to make restitution unless he paid him the freight for the goods, which was contrary to right and a great injury to Thomas unless he had the chancellor's aid.

REQUEST That he would consider that the petitioners had no remedy at common law because of the acquittances, and to grant a writ directed to John Walssh to appear on a given day and under a given penalty to answer in the matter as reason and good conscience demanded, for the love of God etc.

Pledges of prosecution: Thomas Colege, Thomas Aspernine

[1]*Denham*
[2]21 or 29 December

Editor's Note. Allegations of unruly conduct were made against John Walssh, a seaman of Dartmouth, in the complaint of 47 above. He was one of a long list of men—including William Kyd and others accused elsewhere of wrongful seizure of ships—whose arrest had been ordered in 1431, when no reason was given (*CPR 1429–36* p. 132–3, 608). As John Walssh of Dartmouth he was employed by the crown in maritime matters in 1440 (*CPR 1436–41* pp. 413, 451). He was commissioned with others on 28 November 1441 to take bonds of all masters of ships leaving the port of Dartmouth that they would not seize the goods of peaceful subjects of the duke of Brittany, with whom a treaty had lately been concluded (*CPR 1441–6* p. 48). If he had induced the two Breton merchants who were joined with Thomas Roche as petitioners to admit that there had been some justification for seizing their pinnace, perhaps because part of the ship or cargo was French or the crew had shown hostility, his demand for freight for goods returned to Roche would have been in accordance with the customs of the sea governing friends' goods taken in an enemy ship (Introduction p. xiii).

50

C1/71/75

CHANCELLOR The chancellor of England

DATE 1441–2, probably.

PETITIONER Thomas Guychard, merchant of Hennebont[1] in Brittany, joint owner of the *Katherine of Blavet* in Brittany.

COMPLAINT The ship *Katherine of Blavet* of which Nicholas le Galowe was master, and the petitioner and Galahaute Guychard owners, loaded with salt and wine, was on its way to England in the previous June relying on the peace lately made between the king of England and the duke of Brittany, when Thomas Norman and Adam Bole, master and mate[2] of a balinger of Fowey, had seized the ship and goods. Adam Bole had entered it as master and brought it to Fowey and carried off the goods valued at 350 nobles.

The ship had afterwards come into the possession of Richard Edy of Bristol, where it had been arrested by the king's writ, and Richard Edy had been summoned[3] to appear before the chancellor.

REQUEST The petitioner prayed for justice and remedy in the matter as right required, taking into account that Richard Edy was bringing documents[4] from the men of Fowey who had made the capture affirming that the ship was of St. Gilles sur Vie, whereas the petitioner would prove that it was in truth of Brittany. Moreover he feared bodily harm from Richard Edy, and therefore sought a just remedy for God's sake and for charity.

[1]*Henbon*
[2]*countremayster*
[3]*coartyd*
[4]*letters of record*

51a

C1/71/87 *Some words illegible*

CHANCELLOR The chancellor of England

DATE 1441–2

PETITIONER Bertram Godet of Brittany.

COMPLAINT The petitioner had loaded a ship in Brittany with various merchandise intending to discharge it in England at Barnstaple in Devonshire. After he had arrived there Robert Wydeslade of Bideford, Thomas Craddok of Bridgwater and Robert Fuller of Plymouth came and took and imprisoned him and seized the merchandise, alleging that he was a Frenchman, to his great damage and contrary to the truce between England and Brittany.

REQUEST That the chancellor would grant writs of *subpoena* against Robert Wydeslade, Thomas Craddok and Robert Fuller to appear before the chancellor to be examined in the matter as right and conscience required for the love of God etc.

Pledges of prosecution: John Orchard, John Bery, both of county Devon, gentlemen.

51b

C1/43/2

CHANCELLOR The bishop of Bath

DATE 1441–2

PETITIONER Bertram Godet of Brittany.

COMPLAINT The petitioner had recently loaded a ship called the *Maria de Campia* with various merchandise in Brittany, and he, with other seamen in the ship, arrived with the merchandise at Bideford within the port of Barnstaple in Devonshire, expecting to unload it there without hindrance in accordance with the recent truce between the great prince, king Henry VI king of England and John, duke of Brittany. But in Bideford a certain Robert Wydeslade of that town with Thomas Craddok and Robert Fuller came on 27 November 1441 and took the petitioner, and seized and carried away all the merchandise, i.e. 20 tuns of wine valued at £100. They kept the petitioner in prison there, and later in other places, and retained, and were still retaining, all the wine, to his great damage and contrary to the recent truce unless he had the chancellor's aid.

REQUEST That he would consider the matter and grant several writs *subpoena* directed to Robert Wydeslade, Thomas Craddok and Robert Fuller to appear before the chancellor on a day and place and under a penalty to be fixed by him, to be examined concerning the foregoing and all the circumstances, and to give the petitioner sufficient security that they would restore all his merchandise, and damages for his imprisonment and loss of the merchandise, as law and conscience required, in accordance with the truce for the love of God etc.

Pledges of Prosecution: John Burgh, Richard Arnell both 'gentlemen.'

Editor's Note. Petition 51b seems to be an amended version of 51a. Robert Fuller of Plymouth made a recognizance, enrolled on 2 June 1442, promising to pay £40 to Bertram Godet if he failed to abide by the decision of the chancery court in a matter pending between them, or procured his arrest (*CCR 1441–7* p. 79). He was concerned with other complaints of the seizure of ships and goods at this time (below, 52 and Note). Thomas Craddok was the owner of a ship accused of plundering a Spanish ship under safe conduct, captured and taken to Bridgwater in 1443 (*CPR 1441–6*, pp. 201, 247, 287).

52

C1/12/176

CHANCELLOR The bishop of Bath

DATE November 1442–13 May 1443

PETITIONER Richard Clyveden, yeoman of the crown.

COMPLAINT On 28 October 1442, the petitioner's balinger, the *Jaket of Lymington*, seized a barge, the *Marie*, with certain enemy goods in it from La Rochelle, on the high sea as it came out of that port, and brought it to the English coast off Kingsbridge harbour. There, on the following 8 November, Robert Fuller, John Facy, Thomas Power, Richard Lake or Locke, of Plymouth, merchant, Richard Colman of Malborough, weaver, John Vele or Veel, and John Warberton, both merchants of Kingsbridge, John Chilterne of Malborough, labourer, and many others unknown, came with force and arms, i.e.: bows and arrows, spears and swords, on the high sea, and entered the barge, which was in the possession of the petitioner and his men, and took 10 tuns of La Rochelle wine, priced at £4 a tun, a cable, price: 100s., 2 hawsers, price: 4 marks, and 8 oars, price: 12s. 4d., of his goods and chattels and carried them off to Kingsbridge, to his harm and damages of 100 marks.

REQUEST That the chancellor would grant writs *subpoena* directed to Robert Fuller and the others of his company named in this bill at the reverence of God etc.

Editor's Note. The activities of Richard Clyveden (also spelt: Clyfden, Clifden and Cleveden) on the king's business were frequently recorded between 1442 and 1449. Rewards he received for them are also on record. He was given the office of keeper and governor of the king's ships and vessels for life in 1442, to hold himself or by a deputy, at a fee of 12d. a day taken from the customs in the port of Southampton (*CPR 1441–6* pp. 58, 351). In the same year he and two other servants of the king were granted a ship, *La Trinite*, of Bristol, which had been forfeited to the crown, whose right was reserved to take part of the profits of the ship, which were to be accounted for in person by the grantees. He was also granted the office of controller of customs in Southampton in 1445 for good service to the queen. A few months later he was pardoned for offences against the statute of liveries. He had been one of the commissioners appointed in 1444 to inquire into the complaint that a ship owned by Thomas Craddok had captured a Spanish vessel under safe conduct after it had visited Dalkey and sold goods to Dublin merchants (*CPR 1441–6* pp. 39, 58, 351, 356, 396, and above 51 note p. 57).

Robert Fuller of Plymouth—one of the defendants in 51a above—together with other English merchants, took proceedings in chancery in 1442 concerning the capture and plundering in Kingsbridge of a Breton ship and goods by Englishmen which had resulted in the seizure, as reprisal, in Brittany of a balinger of Plymouth—in which presumably he had an interest—and vessels of Cornwall and their cargo. He and John Facy were among the commissioners appointed the following year to inquire into the complaint of the master of the captured Breton ship (*CPR 1441–6* p. 154, 244).

53

C1/16/234 *Slightly damaged, Cited by Kingsford, 1925, p. 91*

CHANCELLOR The archbishop of Canterbury

DATE 1443–4

PETITIONERS Robert Stephyn, Thomas Power of Plymouth, Alyn Furmale and John Purchace of Le Conquet in Brittany.

COMPLAINT The petitioners had recently owned and been in possession of a pinnace called the *Mighell of Dartmouth*, in which they and John Shippeley, John Facy, Richard Lake, Macy Hayes, John Bisshop of Plymouth, Thomas Aisshman, Peter Bere of Plympton and John Beamond of Tavistock had been merchants, with 21 tuns of wine and 17 pieces of linen cloth in it. When the pinnace was sailing from Brittany, bound for Plymouth, a barge called the *Palmer of Fowey*—owned by Haukyn Selaunder, master: Berne Busbas, manned by other robbers and rovers—came out of Plymouth on the Sunday before Christmas 1443 and seized the pinnace with force and arms as it was entering Plymouth harbour, and brought it to Newport in the Isle of Wight. There Thomas Rede of that town received the plunderers and took them in and maintained them in their robbery, and received the wine and goods, valued at [. . .], which he retailed and handled in his house and still retained, to the damage of the petitioners of £40.

REQUEST [That Thomas] Rede might be examined, and the goods or their value restored to them, with damages and costs, for the love of God.

Pledges of prosecution: Robert Fuller of Plymouth. William Fresshepond of Tavistock.

Editor's Note. Two commissions relating to this petition, both dated 28 January 1444, were entered on the patent roll—one to west-country men and the other to men of the Southampton area. In each case the men were appointed to inquire into the complaint of Robert Stephyn and his fellow merchants as set out above, to cause restitution to be made and to imprison those who refused. Nothing further was enrolled (*CPR 1441–46* pp. 246, 247).

54

C1/16/730 *Some words illegible*

CHANCELLOR The archbishop of Canterbury

DATE 1443–5

PETITIONER John Salter

COMPLAINT The petitioner had gone to Fowey in pursuance of a commission directed to him and to Sir Thomas Arundell, Sir John Arundell of

Trerys and John Colege, and had arrested a Breton ship which had been taken by Haukyn Selaunder. Thomas Colan of Bodinnick had come with many others unknown, seamen, intending to murder the petitioner and they were continuing to threaten him; and [. . .] for which he had no remedy against them at common law.

REQUEST That the chancellor would consider the foregoing and grant him a writ *subpoena* directed to Thomas Colan [. . .] him to appear in chancery on a given day to be examined in the matter and to do as good faith and conscience required, and the petitioner would pray to God for the chancellor.

Editor's Note. The commission to which John Salter referred in this petition has not been found on the patent rolls. Sir John Arundell—but not Sir Thomas or Salter himself—was among the commissioners who dealt with complaints about the capture of a Breton ship by Haukyn Selaunder in 1443. Salter was however one of eleven men who were appointed in November 1444 to restore the ship and cargo to the attorneys of its owners after it had come into the possession of Robert Stephen, a Thomas Collan the younger and another man of Bodinnick, and it seems very likely that the threatening behaviour by Thomas Colan complained of above was the result of attempts to carry out these orders (*CPR 1441–6* pp. 244, 246, 338).

55a

C1/45/54 *Badly damaged*

CHANCELLOR The bishop of Bath

DATE 1442–3

PETITIONER Piers Stephan

COMPLAINT An [inquiry], taken before Nicholas [Asshton] and Thomas Bere by virtue of the king's letters patent, and [returned into the] king's chancery, had found that a barge of Nicholas Fevere called the [Marie *of S*]*aint Malo* in Brittany, of which the petitioner was [master], loaded with 43 tuns of wine, priced at 4 marks a tun, had been seized on the high sea by [Nicholas Fric]howe and his confederates and brought to Falmouth in the shire of Cornwall. The inquiry also showed that 14 [tuns of the] wine had come into the hands of Michael [Mul]ner of Dartmouth.

Michael Mulner had afterwards died, whereupon the petitioner had [sued] a writ directed to John Brusshford, mayor of Dartmouth, ordering him to attach Alice, Mulner's wife, executrix and administrator of his goods and chattels, for the restitution of the 14 tuns of wine. The mayor had done so and Alice, being in custody, had delivered £10 worth of pieces of silver and bowls[1] and spoons to the mayor to satisfy the petitioner in part. The mayor, having received the things, let Alice go, and had never returned the writ, nor had he satisfied the petitioner in any way for any part of the 14 tuns of wine, to his great damage and loss without the chancellor's aid.

REQUEST That he would take into consideration his being a foreigner, not able to sue at common law, as well as all the foregoing and to grant a writ *subpoena* directed to John Brusshford mayor of Dartmouth to appear in chancery on a day fixed by the chancellor to answer in the matter, and to bring Alice Mulner with him to answer for the 14 tuns of wine, for the reverence of God etc.

[1]*maseres*

55b

C1/16/24 *French*

CHANCELLOR The archbishop of Canterbury

DATE 1443–4

PETITIONER Piers Stephan

COMPLAINT A writ dated 4 April 1442 had been directed to John Brussh-ford, lately mayor of Dartmouth, to attach and arrest Alice Mulner, widow of Michael Mulner of Dartmouth, and executrix of his will, and also the goods and chattels in Michael's possession in Dartmouth on the day of his death. He was also to produce Alice and the goods at Westminster on the following Ascension day to answer the petitioner in chancery for 14 tuns of white wine, priced at 4 marks sterling a tun, which had come into Michael's hands. It had been part of a cargo of 43 tuns of white wine loaded in a barge, the *Marie of St. Malo*—owner: Nicholas Fever of Nantes, and master: the petitioner—which had been seized by Nicholas Frichowe, Guernak Dutcheman and others, as was fully set out in the return to an inquiry held before Nicholas Asshton and Thomas Bere who had been commissioned with others by the king's letters patent.

The writ had been delivered to John Brusshford on 28 April by John Bailly and Stephen Danyell at Dartmouth, and on its authority John Brusshford, recently mayor, had attached Alice in Dartmouth on the same day, with various goods and chattels belonging to her husband on the day of his death, i.e. several hampers of silver and wooden bowls and silver spoons,[1] valued at £10. After doing this John Brusshford, scheming to cheat the petitioner out of his suit, did not return the writ on the given day, thereby invalidating it.

Alice did not appear in chancery on the given day, and therefore was in default and in contempt of the king,[2] and was hindering the petitioner's suit, to his great damage without the gracious aid of the chancellor.

REQUEST That he would consider the foregoing and grant a writ *subpoena* to John Brusshford to appear in chancery on a given day, and compel him to do what was in accordance with right and conscience, for God etc.

[1]*diverces hanappes dargent maseris et auxi diverce Cuylleris dargent*
[2]*fist defaut a tort et en contempte notre dit Sieur le Roie*

55c

C1/15/12

CHANCELLOR The archbishop of Canterbury

DATE 30 April 1444–Octave of Trinity 1444 or 1445

PETITIONER Piers Stephan, merchant of St. Malo in Brittany.

COMPLAINT The petitioner reminded the chancellor that he had granted him certain writs during the previous Easter term to arrest certain persons of Dartmouth, in particular a *subpoena* of £200 to John Brusshford, mayor of Dartmouth, to appear in chancery at Westminster on the following octave of Trinity, as is shown on the chancery record, to answer the petitioner concerning certain matters which would be put to him.

The writs were delivered to Brusshford in his house on the 30 April by John Lely, gentleman and Robert Bouzemay in the presence of a sergeant. After John Brusshford had pursued them, the sergeant accused John Lely of being a false traitor and thief and ordered him to leave the house at once or he would die there. John Lely, in fear of his life, went away with his company, to his lodging in the town. Shortly afterwards, John Brusshford assembled 400 and more of the commons of the town with pole-axes, swords, spears and bows and arrows who came to the lodging house and assaulted it, intending to kill John Lely and his company. Being prevented from doing so, they set fire to the door and would have burnt it and did much harm, and, but for the grace of God and the help of a priest and another man, John Lely and his men would have been killed and burnt. Such a riot and burning of a house by the king's people is deemed treason in the law.

REQUEST That, at reverence of God, this great and high offence might be punished according to the law and as an example to other wrongdoers, and that the £200 be recovered from John Brusshford if he did not appear in person before the chancellor in chancery at the octave of Trinity, for the benefit of the king and in fulfilment of the chancellor's judgement, for the love of God etc.

55d

C1/17/332

CHANCELLOR The archbishop of Canterbury

DATE 1444–45

PETITIONER Piers Stephan, merchant.

COMPLAINT The petitioner asked the chancellor to consider the great costs, expenses and damages sustained by him as a result of the false return certified into chancery by Nicholas Stebyng, lately mayor of Dartmouth, to certain writs directed to him and the bailiffs of the town, on 26 June 1444 and returnable on the quindene of Michaelmas next following. The writs ordered them to attach John Brusshford[1] of Dartmouth and Alice, widow and executrix of the will of Michael Mullener, so that they should satisfy the petitioner for 14 tuns of white wine, priced at 4 marks a tun, which had been taken at sea with other goods of his, as the chancery record showed. The writs cost 10s., and the expenses and hire of 2 men and 2 horses to ride from London to Dartmouth to deliver them amounted to 100s.

The petitioner sued again later for 3 other writs directed to Nicholas Stebyng and to the bailiffs of the town to attach John Brusshford and Alice, which were returnable on the following octave of Trinity (1445). These cost 10s., and the expenses and hire of 2 men and 2 horses and their labour in delivering them were 100s.

The petitioner's costs and expenses for residing in London during the abovesaid time because of the suit, and for his great delays and damages amounted to £10 and more; to men of law, 13s. 4d., and to the sergeant-at-arms for the arrest of Nicholas Stebyng, 40d.

REQUEST That the chancellor would assess the said sums and modify them at his discretion and advise concerning them so that the petitioner might be duly paid by Nicholas Stebyng, as good conscience required and according to the chancellor's wisdom, for the love of God etc.

[1]Spelt *Brisshford* throughout.

Editor's Note. The years attributed to these four petitions are tentative only since the dates of the writs given by the petitioner and those of the commencement of the archbishop of Canterbury's term as chancellor (13 May 1443) and of the periods when, according to the available information, Brusshford and Stebyng each held office as mayor of Dartmouth (Watkin, 1935, p. 185), cannot be made wholly to agree. It is clear, however, from other evidence that proceedings by Piers Stephan to recover the wine to which he laid claim had begun in 1441: Nicholas Asshton and Thomas Bere, with others, had been appointed to hold inquiries in Cornwall concerning the capture by 3 balingers of Falmouth and Fowey of the barge *Marie of St. Malo* early in that year. On 30 May the sheriff of Cornwall and other commissioners were ordered to cause restitution to be made of her cargo of wine and to imprison all who refused. Asshton and Bere had held their inquiry at Lostwithiel and had found (in addition to the information given by Piers Stephan in the above petitions) that Nicholas Frichowe was the captain of the two balingers of Falmouth and victualler and part owner of them and of another one jointly with five other men, one of whom was Beerun Basebas, i.e. Berne Busbas, master of Haukyn Selaunder's *Palmer of Fowey* 53 above: and that, after bringing the *Marie of St. Malo* to Falmouth, the captors had sold her to six men of various places in Cornwall and Devon who had passed her on to four others. The names were also given of thirteen people, as well as Michael Mulner of Dartmouth, who had each received smaller quantities of the wine than the 14 tuns said to be in his hands. The same information was contained in another commission, issued on 23 October 1441, which ordered the restoration of the ship or its value (£50) to Stephan. This was repeated on 18 August 1442 and on 3 July 1444 (*CPR 1436–41* p. 572 *CPR 1441–46* pp. 47, 106, 288–9). These proceedings had been initiated by Piers Stephan and Nicholas

Fevere together by petition to the king, and Michael Mulner, not his wife,
was named throughout, although according to Stephan's suit against
Brusshford—which was obviously a separate action—he had died before
4 April 1442 (53b above). In July 1444, however, instructions were given
to hold further inquiries to find the value of the property held in Cornwall
by those who refused to make restitution, and to return the result into
chancery on the quindene of the following Michaelmas, It was not until
March 1446 however that still another—this time the last—commission
was enrolled. It indicates that the asked-for inquiries had returned more
up-to-date information about the case since it stated that the 14 tuns of
wine were in Alice's hands, and mentioned only four of the thirteen persons
named in the original inquiry as being still in possession of some of the rest
of it. The commissioners were ordered to arrest them and Alice, to seize
the wine, and also to sell goods of two of the other culprits which were
already in the hands of local officials and to cause restitution to be made
to Piers Stephan or his attorney, and, as before, to imprison all who refused
and, in addition, to inquire into their lands and goods (*CPR 1441–46*
p. 423).

56

C1/45/399

CHANCELLOR The bishop of Bath and Wells

DATE 23 May 1433–13 May 1443

PETITIONERS John Barell and Martin Treher of the shire of Cornwall,
merchants.

COMPLAINT The petitioners had delivered certain merchandise to their
attorney, Hugh Mighelstowe, to take from Cornwall to Ireland to trade.
He had arrived there at Waterford, where John Mourton, clerk, parson of
the church of Ilfracombe in Devonshire, had come to him and told him
that he had lately been taken at sea by the king's enemies and put to ransom[1] for a great sum and set on land in a strange country where he had no
friends. He had begged Hugh Mighelstowe to help him with £40 in money
to pay his ransom, and the latter, seeing that he was in great distress,
agreed to help him provided that he would be bound in an obligation of
£40 to him and to John Skyle, master of the ship which Hugh was in.
John Mourton agreed, whereupon Hugh delivered £40 worth of the goods
of the petitioners to him. John Mourton had written an obligation, in his
own hand, to pay the sum of £40 to Hugh and John Skyle within ten days
of the coming to England of his servant, William Lytylton, as appeared
more plainly in the obligation. Later, John Mourton came to John Skyle
and persuaded him to make a general release with the intention of barring
Hugh Mighelstowe from an action at law, and gave his hand that he
would pay him 40s. in cash[2] if he would do so. John Skyle, not knowing of
the obligation, had taken the 40s. and made an acquittance of all manner
of personal actions which would prevent the petitioners from claiming the
£40.

REQUEST That the chancellor would consider the foregoing and send a writ after John Mourton to appear before him in chancery on a day and under a penalty to be fixed by him to be examined in the matter, and give judgement on the examination so that the petitioners be satisfied for their £40 and for the damages which they had suffered in the matter, for the love of God etc.

Pledges of prosecution: John Rem, Richard Love.

[1]*fynance*
[2]*and bare an hand he shuld pay him XLs of money*

Editor's Note. The petitioner in this case was, no doubt, the John Barell who was one of the commissioners appointed on 30 May 1441 to cause restitution to be made to Piers Stephan of the cargo of the *Marie of St. Malo*, and the John Barill of Penryn named in the commission enrolled on 25 March 1446 (above 55 note p. 64). There is a reference to ' John Morton, clerk', with lands and chattels and church goods in Devonshire dated 8 November 1429 (*CCR 1429-36* p. 26).

57

CI/15/183

CHANCELLOR The archbishop of Canterbury.

DATE 13 May 1443-31 January 1450

PETITIONER John Legodek of Penmarch in Brittany, owner of a ship, *St. Trevers of Penmarch*, 54 tontight.[1]

COMPLAINT The petitioner was in his ship, freighted with salt, when it was taken at sea by sea rovers[2] and brought by them to Fowey and there sold to Thomas Clerk of Ireland. He on his way back to Ireland, was driven by storm into Mount's Bay. The petitioner went there and claimed his ship and freight, but had not yet obtained restitution of them. They were being kept under arrest by the sheriff of Cornwall.

REQUEST That the chancellor would grant a commission to Thomas Bere, Thomas Trefrey and John Salter to inquire into the matter, and to restore the ship and freight to him in accordance with what they found, for the love of God etc.

[1]*tunetight* i.e. tonnage.
[2]*Bremers*, i.e. scumers or scourers of the sea, or sea rovers.

Editor's Note. The commission sought by John Legodek does not appear on the patent roll. Thomas Trefrey had been employed by the crown and on commissions in 1432-3 and he and Thomas Bere and John Salter all served on commissions between 1441 and 1446, and held offices in Devon and Cornwall during that period (above, 29 and note p. 32, 55a and note p. 63, *CCR 1441-47* p. 148, *CPR 1441-46* p. 206, 274, 339). All three, or men with the same names, were still serving in the fourteen-fifties (*CPR 1452-61* passim).

58

C1/15/223

CHANCELLOR The archbishop of Canterbury.

DATE 13 May 1443–31 January 1450

PETITIONER William Nerbere of St. Athan in Glamorgan South Wales.

COMPLAINT Thomas Gower, captain of Cherbourg and John Bere of
Barnstaple in Devonshire were in possession and owners of a balinger
called the *Mary*. Thomas Gower granted his part of the ship to the petitioner who had been peaceably in possession of it, by reason of the grant,
in common with John Bere; until William Lethycote, also of Barnstaple,
was allowed by John Bere to enter wrongfully into the petitioner's part of
the ship, and had kept it wrongfully from him for more than 6 years, and
was still doing so, to his great harm.

REQUEST That the chancellor would consider the foregoing and grant a
writ of *subpoena* directed to William Lethycote, commanding him to appear
on a given day before the king in chancery to answer the petitioner in the
matter, so that the latter might recover his part of the ship and the damages
he had sustained in accordance with the chancellor's wisdom, as good
conscience and reason required, for the love of God.

Pledges of prosecution: William Hunt, John Thomas.

59

C1/124/26

CHANCELLOR The archbishop of Canterbury

DATE 13 May 1443–2 March 1454

PETITIONER John Cayphas, merchant of Guerande in Brittany.

COMPLAINT A writ *subpoena* of £400 had been directed recently by the
chancellor to John Darundell, esquire, of Cornwall, and also an order
under privy seal commanding him on his allegiance to deliver to the
petitioner the ship called the *Grymole of Guerande* with all its gear. He had
arrested it contrary to the form of the treaty of peace between the king of
England and the duke of Brittany. The petitioner had hired John More,
sergeant-at-arms, to ride to Cornwall and deliver the writ and privy seal.
When John Darundell had heard of the sergeant-at-arms' approach he
withdrew from place to place to prevent the execution of the writ and
privy seal, to the great delay and damage and costs of the petitioner
unless he had the chancellor's present help in the matter.

REQUEST That, at the reverence of God, he would grant a commission
directed to Sir William Bonevyle, the sheriff of Cornwall and John More,
sergeant-at-arms, giving them power, jointly or separately, to deliver the

ship and its gear to the petitioner wherever it should be found without any delay. And also to arrest John Brown of Cornwall 'beside the Fowey,' for 23 ' *salutz* ' for salt of the petitioner's which he had received from the ship, and to commit him to prison until restitution had been made to the petitioner for the sum as right required, so that he had no cause to complain further in the matter and in fulfilment of the chancellor's judgement, for the love of God etc.

Editor's Note. The requested commission cannot be found on the patent roll. The archbishop of Canterbury was chancellor from 1443 till 1450 and again from July 1452 till 1454. During this period John More received a grant of 12d. a day from the customs of Ipswich to date from 17 December 1444 in lieu of wages for the office of sergeant-at-arms (*CPR 1446–52*, p. 149) and there are frequent references to him on the business of the crown. Sir William Bonevyle and John Darundell were also so employed. (Ibid, *passim*, and below 64 and 65 notes pp. 70, 71).

60

C1/17/381

CHANCELLOR The archbishop of Canterbury.

DATE 13 May 1443–31 January 1450

PETITIONER John Stevens

COMPLAINT The petitioner had been at sea in a carvel of Fowey, when it took a Breton prize, and, much against his will, he had been put in it to guide it, on condition that if it were re-captured the whole company of the carvel would pay his ransom. Soon afterwards the prize was re-captured and brought to Brittany, and the petitioner had been made, and still was, a prisoner. Although Michael de la Mote of Bodinnick in Cornwall had collected the ransom for his release from the company in accordance with the agreement, he was keeping it and allowing the petitioner to remain in prison in Brittany to his complete undoing unless he had the chancellor's aid.

REQUEST That he would consider the foregoing and how the petitioner had no remedy at common law, and grant a writ *subpoena* directed to Michael de la Mote to appear in the king's Chancery on a given day to be examined about the foregoing, and to do whatever right and conscience required in the matter for the love of God etc.

Editor's Note. A John Steven or Stevenes was commissioned to arrest ships and men for the victualling of the castle of Le Crotoy between 1441 and 1443 (*CPR 1441–6* pp. 80, 245).

Michael de la Mote was one of the owners and victuallers of a balinger of Fowey which was accused in 1453 of taking the *St. Ives of St. Malo* when it was sailing to England under letters of safe conduct (below 64).

61

C1/19/483

CHANCELLOR The cardinal archbishop of York

DATE 31 January 1450—21 July 1452

PETITIONER Henry, duke of Exeter.

COMPLAINT On Whit Monday 1449, in Plymouth in the county of Devonshire, two French men, Piers Bakeston and Piers Chasault of Limousin,[1]
enemies of the king, were taken by the duke's servant, Thomas Ayton, and
gave themselves up and became prisoners of the duke, and were accepted
on his behalf by Thomas Ayton. Later, on the following 12 July, in South-
hampton, Thomas Ayton, by order of Master Hugh Payn, also a servant
of the duke, delivered the two prisoners to Peryn Baker and William
Romond to keep on the duke's behalf. They had kept them in their
custody until 7 October 1449, when Thomas and John Payn of Southampton forcibly removed them from their keeping for the benefit of the
mayor, sheriff, bailiffs and commonalty of Southampton.

REQUEST That the chancellor would examine the prisoners and Peryn
Baker and William Romond openly in chancery upon the foregoing, and
ordain and award that the prisoners should be restored to the duke as right
and conscience required.

[1]*Lemosyn'*

Editor's Note. Henry, duke of Exeter, had succeeded his father, John, by
March 1448, before he was of age, and had been in the king's wardship.
He received licence to enter his possessions in July 1450. Both he and his
father held the office of admiral of England. Complaints were made
against Master Hugh Payn, the lieutenant of each of them, concerning
irregularities in the admiralty court (*CPR 1446–52* pp. 63, 142, 146, 333,
417, 564).
    Thomas Ayton was a servant of the household of Henry, duke of Exeter
in 1450 (*CCR 1447–54* p. 145). In the same year John Payn (who was
mayor of Southampton in 1451) and Thomas Payn were appointed to
arrest wine and woad and deliver it to a man of Bordeaux since there had
been no response to a proclamation, made in Southampton, that anyone
who knew of a reason why this should not be done should appear in
chancery on a given date (*CPR 1446–52* p. 432, 442).

62

C1/19/3

CHANCELLOR The cardinal of York [sic]

DATE 31 January 1450–21 July 1452

PETITIONER John Pappaye

COMPLAINT The petitioner had loaded certain packs of cloth in a barge,
the *Trinity of Falmouth*, John Bodye at the time owner, at Plymouth for

Lisbon, and John Bodye and some of his seamen broke the packs and took away cloth worth 20 marks. For this offence, the petitioner, rightfully sued an action of trespass against John Bodye, whereupon the latter, out of malice and without cause, affirmed a plant of trespass against the petitioner in London which had been brought up into the chancery court by a *corpus cum causa*.

REQUEST That the chancellor would consider the foregoing and discharge him of the feigned suit and dismiss him from the court at the reverence of God etc.

63

C1/22/10 *Some words illegible*

CHANCELLOR The cardinal archbishop of Canterbury

DATE 21 July 1452–2 March 1454

PETITIONER Piers Mountier, merchant and subject of the sovereign lord of the isle of Guernsey.

COMPLAINT Recently, on 9 June 1450 John Girdeller of the neighbourhood of Budleigh in the shire of Devonshire, master of a balinger of the city of Exeter of which William atte Wylle, Thomas Kelly, of the same city, and John Hakeworthy of Exe Island in the same shire were owners and victuallers, together with [. . .] and wrongdoers, captured the petitioner's pinnace, *Courtabelle*, with goods of his, i.e. 40 pieces of crece, 4 pieces of small cloth, one thousand canvasses and other goods valued at £100 sterling, with force and against the king's peace on the high sea near Guernsey to the utter undoing of the petitioner without the chancellor's aid.

REQUEST That the chancellor would consider the foregoing and that the poor merchants, the inhabitants of the aforesaid isle, and their ancestors were, and always had been, true subjects of the king and his forefathers and under their rule since the conquest, and grant the king's writs addressed severally to John Girdeller, William atte Wylle, Thomas Kelly and John Hakeworthy to appear before the king in chancery on the morrow of St. John, each under a penalty of £100, to answer the king and to the petitioner concerning the foregoing for the love of God etc.

64

C1/22/57

CHANCELLOR The cardinal archbishop of Canterbury

DATE 21 July 1452–16 June 1453

PETITIONER John Valanson, merchant of Brittany.

COMPLAINT The statute made in parliament at Westminster in 1353 provided, among other things, that any merchant, native or foreign, robbed of his goods on the sea might, if they came to any part of the realm, recover them on proof that they were his by his cocket, mark, letters, charter parties or other reasonable proof without a suit at common law. The petitioner had been granted letters of safe conduct by the king for a ship called *St. Yves of St. Malo* in Brittany, of 100 tons or less, and his goods and merchandise, and adequate masters and seamen, and had loaded 70 tuns of wine and 10 tons of iron, valued at £700 and more, in the ship by his factors; and it and the goods had been taken on the high sea on the way to England by John Harle, master of a balinger, the *Nicholas of Fowey*, whose owners and victuallers were John Harle, Richard Nottes, Michael de la Motte, Thomas Burgate, Henry Snayleham, Walter Poole and Richard Beddwyn, and quartermasters, Henry Snayleham, Philip Bocher, Richard Nottes and John Hoore, and by Haukyn Drake, master of a vessel called a *Barke*, owners and victuallers, Edmund Kendall, priest, Richard Kendall, Thomas Burgate, John Cornewe, John Broun, goldsmith, and Laurence Bereman. They had brought the *St. Yves* into the port of Fowey in the county of Cornwall and plundered the ship and goods there, and divided them amongst themselves and others unknown to the petitioner, to his great loss and damages unless he had a suitable remedy.

REQUEST That the chancellor would consider the foregoing and that he had no remedy at the common law of the land, and grant writs of *subpoena* to each of the owners and victuallers of the ship, *Nicholas of Fowey* and the *Barke* commanding them to appear before the king in chancery on a certain day under heavy penalties to be fixed by the chancellor to answer the charges and to make amends as good faith and conscience required. And further that the petitioner may have commissions directed to well known people to be chosen by the chancellor to inquire into the foregoing and to cause proper restitution of the goods to be made in whose-ever hands they were found.

And also that the chancellor should intercede with the king for letters of privy seal to be addressed to each of the wrongdoers ordering them to appear before him and his council to answer to the foregoing. For the love of God etc.

Editor's Note. William Bonevile of Chewton and John Colshull, both knights, the sheriff of Cornwall and three others were commissioned on 16 June 1453 to hold an inquiry in Cornwall concerning the complaint, to discover who was guilty, the value of the ship and merchandise, and into whose hands they had come, and to make restitution to the petitioner. (*CPR 1452–61* p. 119 and cp. above, 59). More than two years later William Bonevile, with John Arundell, esquire, was appointed to arrest all the men complained of by the petitioner, except Michael de la Motte and Richard Kendall, and to bring them before the king in chancery to answer certain charges (*CPR 1452–61* p. 258).

65

C1/22/14 *Badly damaged. Illegible words supplied from CPR 1452–61 p. 118.*

CHANCELLOR The cardinal archbishop of Canterbury

DATE 21 July 1452–5 June 1453

PETITIONER Philip Mede, merchant of Bristol.

COMPLAINT The king, at the prayer of Peter[Seynt] Cryke, esquire, born in [Aquitaine], had recently taken under his safe conduct and protection, by letters patent dated 17 June 1452, a ship of Spain of [. . .] tons or less with goods and merchandise and merchants and [crew] numbering 60 people. Relying on the safe conduct, the petitioner had loaded 80 tons of iron, wood and other merchandise of great [value] in a ship of Spain called *Seynt Cruce*. This ship was sailing on the sea, with the safe conduct, towards Bristol when Thomas Adam of Polruan, master of a ship called the *Palmer*, Robert Hikkes [of Polruan, Thomas Philip and Hohn Huyssh, merchant, owners and] victuallers, and John Huyssh, seamen, master of a ship called *la Julyan of Fowey*, John Atterede and Walter Hill, priest, owners and victuallers, with many others, arrayed for war, came and took it by force on the high seas with the goods and merchandise belonging to the petitioner, factor and attorney of Peter [Seynt Cryke], and brought them to the port of Fowey where they intended to treat them as their own to the petitioner's great loss and damage without [the chancellor's aid].

REQUEST That the chancellor would consider the foregoing and that the petitioner was ready to prove that the goods and merchandise belonged to him [in accordance with] the statute providing for such a case, and to grant writs *subpoena* directed to Thomas Adam, and to each of the men named above, commanding them, under heavy penalties, to appear in person before the king in chancery on a day fixed by the chancellor to answer to the foregoing, and [to do as good faith and conscience required]. And he asked also that a commission directed to certain impartial persons should be granted to inquire into the foregoing [and to cause restitution to be made] for the love of God etc.

Editor's Note. The petitioner, Philip Mede, was becoming prominent in Bristol at this time, he was frequently on commissions to deal with complaints about captured ships and goods (Veale, Text I and II *passim*, CPR *1452–61* pp. 60, 225, 438, 495, 517, 608).

A commission was issued on 5 June 1453, to six named men, including Sir William Bonevile and John Arundell, esquire, and to the sheriff of Cornwall authorising them to hold an inquiry in the county to find who had been responsible for the capture and detention of the *Seynt Cruce* and her cargo, the value of the ship and goods, and into whose hands they had come; and to make restitution in accordance with statute 2 Henry V. (CPR *1452–61* p. 118).

Thomas Adam of Polruan was among those accused of capturing a Genoese carrack sailing from Spain to England, and taking it to Fowey in 1433 (above, 33).

66

C1/22/93

CHANCELLOR The cardinal archbishop of Canterbury

DATE 21 July 1452–2 March 1454

PETITIONERS Thomas and Robert Bray

COMPLAINT The petitioners had recently seized a ship of Brittany, with 18 Bretons and a cargo of 75 tuns of wine and other goods valued at £500, and brought them to the harbour of Topsham. But there the bailiff, William atte Welle, took the Bretons and the wine and goods out of the petitioners' custody by virtue of a safe conduct which had been granted for the ship by the admiral of England, and let them go at large, to the petitioners' utter undoing without the chancellor's aid.

REQUEST That he would consider the foregoing and grant a writ *subpoena* directed to William atte Welle to appear before the king in chancery on a certain day, to be examined concerning the matter and to do and receive what conscience [and good faith] required, for the love of God etc.

Pledges of prosecution: Edward Bray of Abingdon, Berkshire, merchant. John Walker of Standlake, Oxfordshire.

Editor's Note. The petitioners, described as of Abingdon, had been granted letters of marque and reprisals, dated July 1449, against the subjects of the duke of Brittany as a result of a complaint by them stating that they had shipped merchandise valued at 1000 marks to Brittany, in time of truce, and sold it to Breton merchants and received payment at their house in St. Servan near St. Malo. They had left the goods there in the care of Thomas Bray's apprentice while they had gone elsewhere in Brittany for money owed to them by other merchants. During their absence Robert Pountevale, lieutenant of the castle of Celidorte in Brittany, assisted by the keeper of the house and others had murdered the apprentice and divided the goods among themselves. The petitioners, on their return, had sued the culprits and received judgement for the recovery of 1000 marks, but had not obtained execution of the judgement (*CPR 1446–52* p. 257).

67a

C1/24/261 *Many words illegible. Printed in full by Kingsford, 1925, pp. 180–1.*

CHANCELLOR The earl of Salisbury

DATE 5 January–7 March 1455

PETITIONER William Mayhewe, citizen and fishmonger of London.

COMPLAINT The petitioner's ship, the *John of Calais*, loaded with his goods, total value £300, was being held under arrest by the bishop of St. Andrews in Scotland as a reprisal for the ship, *Marie of St. Andrews*, which, loaded with the bishop's wine and other merchandise, had been captured at sea by westcountry men towards the end of 1453, contrary to the king's peace and the truce between Henry VI and the king of Scotland, and for which no restitution had been received. The ship and its cargo had, however, been claimed as his own property by a William Kanete, knight, posing as the bishop's brother who had obtained a commission directed to the west-country men to make restitution of them to him. On the strength of this he had received the ship and part of the merchandise in the west country, and had sold the ship to Thomas Gylle. The bishop of St. Andrews had been informed of this in writing, and had declared that Sir William was not his brother, or owner of the ship and merchandise, and had sent the petitioner a written statement to this effect. Whereupon the latter had sued to the chancellor, who had issued a commission to the king's officers in Sandwich, where the ship lay in harbour, appointing them to arrest it. But the men in her at the time resisted the arrest, threatening the lives of the commissioners if they so much as touched the ship, so that they returned home in fear, and the ship and freight escaped from the harbour. Therefore the petitioner could not obtain the release of his ship, the *John of Calais*, which was being held in Scotland, in his utter undoing without the chancellor's aid.

REQUEST That the chancellor would consider the foregoing and grant several writs *subpoena* to Thomas Gylle, and to the sheriff of Devon and John Nedam, master of the *Marie* at the time of the attempted arrest, ordering them to bring the ship and freight to [. . .]; and also to appear before the chancellor and other lords of the king's council, under a penalty etc.

67b

C1/24/5 *Printed in full by Kingsford, 1925, pp. 181–2*

THOMAS GYLLE'S[1] ANSWER TO THE BILL SUED AGAINST HIM BY WILLIAM MAYHEWE,[2] CITIZEN AND FISHMONGER OF LONDON.

Thomas Gylle said that the bill did not contain any wrong, trespass or offence committed by him against William Mayhewe to be answered, and prayed to be discharged and dismissed from the court of chancery.

He declared that the truth was that he had known nothing of the false claim which Sir William Kanete was alleged to have made to the *Marie of St. Andrews* and its cargo by reason of which he had obtained possession of them after they had been unlawfully taken by west-country men. Thomas Gylle, Sir William Bourghier of Fitzwaryn, knight, Nicholas Aissheton, and others had been commissioned by letters patent dated 3 July 1454 to inquire into the taking of the ship, and to restore it to Sir William Kanete as appeared more plainly in the copies of the commission and the return to it which were attached to this answer.[3] Since Sir William Kanete had recovered the ship and goods as a result of the commission and the evidence brought before it, Thomas Gylle had not been party to any offence or wrong, and prayed to be dismissed out of the chancery court.

[1]Spelt *Gille* throughout
[2]Spelt *Mayowe*
[3]Below 67d and e

67c

C1/24/6 *Printed in full, Kingsford, 1925, p. 182*

WILLIAM MAYHEWE'S REPLICATION TO THOMAS GYLLE'S REJOINDER.

William Mayhewe said that Thomas Gylle had known that the ship, *Marie of St. Andrews*, and its cargo had belonged rightfully to the bishop of St. Andrews, both at the time it was taken and when it was delivered to Sir William Kanete. He said also that Thomas Gylle and Sir William had contrived together to obtain the commission and the inquiry and examination in order that the ship and its contents should be delivered to Sir William and so that Thomas Gylle should buy them at his own price, as had been set out in William Mayhewe's earlier replication to Thomas Gylle's answer.[1]

And Thomas Gylle had not denied that he knew that the ship had been taken unlawfully contrary to the king's safe conduct, which was the reason why William Mayhewe's ship, *John of Calais*, had been taken to, and was being kept in, Scotland; therefore he prayed that Thomas Gylle should be compelled to make restitution of the *Marie of St. Andrews* to the bishop of St. Andrews, so that William Mayhewe might have recovery of the *John of Calais* and of his goods. He was ready to prove all that he had said in whatever way the court awarded and therefore prayed judgement etc.

[1]Mayhewe's replication (following Gylle's answer) and Gylle's rejoinder have not survived.

67d

C1/24/4 *Latin CPR 1452–61 p. 178*

COMMISSION to Sir William Bourghier de Fitzwaryn, knight, Nicholas Aissheton, Sir Philip Courtney, knight, Sir John Denham, knight, Thomas Gylle, James Chudley and Nicholas Radford, on the complaint of Sir William Kanete of Scotland, knight, that William Kydde and other pirates had seized his ship, *le Marie of St. Andrews*, loaded with various merchandise, and taken it to Devon. The commissioners were to hold inquiries as to who was guilty, and who was in possession of the ship and goods and to arrest the latter and restore them to William Kanete or to his attorneys, John Ecton and John Staple; and to imprison those who refused to make restitution. Dated 3 July 1454.

67e

Ci/24/3 *Latin*

CERTIFICATE MADE IN PURSUANCE OF THE COMMISSION ISSUED 3 JULY 1454.

James Chudley, Nicholas Radford and Thomas Gylle, three of the commissioners, made certificates at Exeter on 10 August 1454, by the testimony of John Germyn, mayor of Exeter, John Coteler, John Beaufitz, citizens of Exeter and others, that the ship of William Kanete of Scotland, knight, with his goods and merchandise was at Exmouth on that date in the custody of William Kydde, and that they had seized the ship and merchandise and delivered them to William Kanete as directed in the letters patent.

They also certified that neither by the inquiry nor in any other way could they discover who were the pirates who had captured the ship with William Kydde; and that William Kydde had not been found in the county of Devonshire between the delivery to them of the letters patent and their return.

Editor's Note. The earliest reference to the *Marie of St. Andrews* was a commission issued on 14 March 1454, at the request of King James of Scotland, appointing the sheriff of Devon, Sir Philip Courtney and Sir John Denham to make inquiries into the taking during a truce of the ship, which had letters of safe conduct, and its cargo and to imprison the culprits until they made restitution. Neither the bishop of St. Andrews or Sir William Kanete nor any other owner was mentioned. The commission of 3 July 1454—of which 67d is a copy—and the certificate, 67e, followed and resulted in the delivery of the ship and merchandise to William Kanete and to the proceedings described by William Mayhewe in his petition, 67a. The commission to the king's officers in Sandwich had been enrolled on 5 January 1455. The petition 67a and the pleadings to it resulted in another commission in December 1455 to Sir Philip Courtney, the sheriff of Devon and eight others setting out all the facts given in the previous documents, stating that Sir William Kanete's suit had been fraudulent, and appointing the commissioners as usual to hold inquiries, imprison the guilty, and compel restitution to be made, if necessary by distraint on the goods of those in possession of the ship and cargo.

William Mayhewe and a John Batte of Calais, who had been appointed by the bishop of St. Andrews as his proctors to sue in chancery for the recovery of the ship, later stated in court that the ship and its tackle had been arrested at Dartmouth by five of the commissioners. The proctors obtained an order early in the following March, to four of the same men with the sheriff of Devon again, and the mayor and water bailiff of Dartmouth to deliver the ship to themselves and to protect them on leaving the port. The commissioners were, however, prevented from carrying out these instructions because the man then in possesson of the ship—the name of which had been changed first to the *Marie of Dartmouth* and then to the *Antony of Dartmouth*—had obtained a licence to take it with thirty pilgrims to Santiago in Galicia. The same commissioners received further orders in April to restore the ship to William Mayhewe and John Batte, which seems to have brought the matter to a close (*CPR 1452–61* p. 170, 178, 224, 301, 303. Kingsford pp. 89–90).

68

C1/25/54

CHANCELLOR The archbishop of Canterbury

DATE 12 November 1455

PETITIONER Otys Treunwyth and Joce Hamell

COMPLAINT The petitioners had affirmed a plaint of debt in the franchise court of the provost of Eton at St. Michael's Mount[1] in the shire of Cornwall before Richard Penpons, then steward, against Piers Kesseron, John Balyn and Laurens Erbras, all three of Brittany, demanding £24, whereupon Piers, John and Laurens were attached by 24 tuns of wine, which had been put in to the keeping of Thomas Favy, officer of the court, to satisfy the petitioners if judgement was in their favour. Piers, John and Laurens had appeared in the court by force of this attachment, and the petitioners had declared against them, demanding the sum of £24 for a ship and one prisoner which they had sold to the defendants, as the latter admitted so that the petitioners had received judgement that they should recover the debt with damages of 20s. But after judgement, and before it could be executed, Mychell Uty, Baudyn Laury, and John Ronolt' of Marckolsheim[2] with other wrongdoers carried off the wine, preventing the execution of the judgement, to the petitioner's great damage, injury[3] and undoing without the chancellor's aid in the matter.

REQUEST That he would consider the foregoing and grant several writs of *subpoena* directed to Michell Uty, Baudyn Laury and John Ronolt' to appear in chancery on a day fixed by him to be examined in the foregoing, and to award as the law and conscience required, for the love of God etc.

Latin Memorandum that on 12 November 1455 James Flamank' of Boscastle[4] in the county of Cornwall, knight, and Martin Penpons of Trewithen in the same county, gentleman, mainperned before the king in chancery for Otys and Joce that if they could not prove the matter in their petition to be true, then they would satisfy Michell, Baudewin and John for all the damages and expenses which they had sustained in this action in accordance with the provisions of the statute.[5]

[1] *the Mounte*
[2] *Markheisen*
[3] *hurtyng*
[4] *Boscarne*
[5] See Introduction p. xviii

Editor's Note. Richard Penpons and Otto and Peter Treunwith, with John Harry, were named as victuallers and in possession, with others, of *le Katerine of St. Ives*, manned by Englishmen, who had on 30 October 1452 seized the *George of Dartmouth*, recently owned by Thomas Gille and bought by Peter and John Adam of London, on its way from Lisbon to London loaded with goods and merchandise of the two Adams and men of Portugal. An inquiry held before Sir William Bonevile, John Colshull and the sheriff of Cornwall during the following year found that Penpons, Otto

Treunwith and John Harry had received the merchandise from the *George of Dartmouth*, and a later inquiry, held before Bonevile, Nicholas Asshton and one other, at Launceston, named the men who had been in the *Katerine* at the time of the capture and revealed that Richard Penpons of Trewithen, gentleman, was owner and victualler of half the ship, and eleven named men (seven of them of St. Ives including Peter Treunwith) of the other half, and also named ten men of other places in Cornwall as being in possession of part of the goods (*CPR 1452–61* pp. 61, 165, 174).

Other evidence suggests that Richard Penpons, who was on a number of commissions at this time and was a J.P., was also an unscrupulous supporter of Cornish sea rovers (No. 69 and 72 below).

69

C1/25/121

CHANCELLOR The archbishop of Canterbury

DATE 12 November 1455

PETITIONER Thomas Geffray of Portreath.[1]

COMPLAINT The petitioner had affirmed a plaint of debt before Richard Penpons, steward of the franchise court of the provost of Eton at St. Michael's Mount[2] in the shire of Cornwall, against William Coke of Bodinnick[3] demanding 47 marks for certain contracts made between them, whereupon William Coke had been attached by a ship loaded with 20 tuns of wine which had been put into the keeping of Thomas Favy, officer of the court, to satisfy the petitioner if judgement was in his favour. William Coke had appeared in court by force of this attachment, and the petitioner had declared against him demanding the said sum for certain merchandise which he had sold to the defendant as the latter could not deny, whereupon the petitioner had received judgement that he should recover the said sum and damages of 20s. But after judgement and before it could be executed, William Clemowe and many other wrongdoers came and carried off the ship, loaded with wine, preventing the execution of the judgement, to the petitioner's great damage, injury[4] and undoing without the chancellor's aid in the matter.

REQUEST That he would consider the foregoing and grant a writ of *subpoena* directed to William Clemowe to appear in chancery on a day fixed by him to be examined in the foregoing, and to award as the law and conscience required, for the love of God etc.

Memorandum (in exactly the same terms as in 68) that on 12 November 1455, James Flamank and Martin Penpons of Trewithen mainperned for the petitioner that he would satisfy William Clemowe for his damages and expenses if he was not able to prove the truth of the matter in the petition.

[1] *Porthea*
[2] *the Mount*
[3] *Bodynnacke*
[4] *hurtyng*

Editor's Note. This petition as well as the memorandum is drawn up in identical terms as 68 above. Thomas Geffray and William Coke each had interests—the one as owner the other as victualler—in carvels of Fowey which captured a Spanish ship in the summer of 1457 (*CPR 1452–61* p. 441).

70a

C1/25/207

CHANCELLOR The archbishop of Canterbury

DATE 7 March 1455–11 October 1456

PETITIONER Edmund Mulso, knight.

COMPLAINT Geoffrey Garvey, a servant of the petitioner, had loaded the latter's ship, the *Mary of Dublin*[1] in Ireland, capacity[2] 70 tons, at Dublin to come to London with the petitioner's goods, particulars of which appeared in a schedule attached to this bill.[3] During the journey, on 26 November 1451, Thomas Bodulgate, esquire, in another ship with many other persons arrayed for war, had met the *Mary of Dublin* on the high sea and entered it by force and without warrant and had taken command of it and all its tackle, valued at £100, and had taken possession of all the petitioner's goods, not allowing Geoffrey or any of his seamen to attend to[4] either ship or goods. Having seized the ship and goods in this way, he had taken them to Fowey in Cornwall and detained them there, withholding them from the petitioner contrary to right and conscience and to his injury and loss of £400 without the chancellor's aid.

REQUEST That he would consider the foregoing and grant a writ of *subpoena* directed to Thomas Bodulgate commanding him to appear before the king in chancery on a day given by the chancellor to answer the foregoing, and to compel him to deliver the ship and goods to the petitioner in accordance with the statute provided for such a case and to abide by the award of the court; and the petitioner would pray to God for the chancellor.

[1]*Debelyn*
[2]*of the portage of*
[3]*Below,* 70b
[4]*melle*

70b

C1/25/208A *Attached schedule*

First: 6½ lasts of hides, price: 41 marks 8s. 10d. the last. Sum £86 13s. 3d.[1]
Item: 7½ hundred of Irish frieze, price: £3 the hundred. Sum £22 10s.

Item: 80 mantles of Ireland, price 4s. the piece. Sum £16.

Item: 2 pipes and a hogshead and 2 barrels of molten tallow[2] of the value of £12.

Item: a prisoner of Brittany who was ransomed to £20.

[1]These seem to be the figures in the original document, which are written quite clearly
[2]*molten talogh*

70c

C1/25/208B

This is the answer of Thomas Bodulgate, esquire, to the bill of Edmund Mulso, knight.

The answer recites Edmund Mulso's complaint word for word as given in the bill i.e. that Thomas Bodulgate with others arrayed for war had entered and taken command of his ship, which with its tackle was valued at £100, and had seized all the goods in it and had refused to allow Geoffrey Garvey or his seamen to touch them or the ship, and had taken them to Fowey and was detaining them from Edmund Mulso. To which Thomas Bodulgate said by protestation that the ship, tackle and goods were never of the value given in the bill.

And he also said that the matter in the bill was determinable by common law and insufficient to require him to answer in the chancery court. And for answer he denied that he had met Edmund's ship on the high sea or entered it with force, or taken it and the goods and brought them to Fowey, or was detaining them or any part of them as alleged in the bill. And he said also that the ship, tackle and goods were not owned at the time of the alleged taking by Edmund Mulso, but belonged to Piers Clinton, Richard Palmer and Geoffrey Garvey. And Thomas Bodulgate was ready to prove all this in whatever way the court awarded.

Therefore he prayed to be dismissed from the court with his costs and damages.

70d

C1/25/208C

This is the replication of Edmund Mulso, knight, to the answer of Thomas Bodulgate, esquire.

First as to Thomas Bodulgate's statement in his answer that ship, tackle and goods were owned by Piers Clynton, Richard Palmer and Geoffrey Garvey at the time of the alleged taking and not to Edmund Mulso, he said that their ownership was his at that time, as he had submitted in his bill, as he was ready to prove in whatever way the court awarded.

And as to the remainder of Thomas Bodulgate's answer, Edmund said by protestation that he denied that any part of it was true, but for replication to it said that no law required him to answer it in the manner and form in which it had been made.

Therefore he asked for judgement for default of answer by Thomas Bodulgate, and prayed that he might recover his ship, tackle and goods, and damages in accordance with the terms of the statute provided in such a case or their value, as right and conscience required.

Editor's Note. No orders connected with this complaint were enrolled. References to Edmund Mulso are to a knight of the counties of Northampton and Suffolk, and associated in one of them with citizens of London (*CCR 1447–54* p. 504; see also Ibid. p. 238, 400 and *CPR 1446–52* pp. 130, 233).

Thomas Bodulgate was one of the influential men of Cornwall who was constantly employed on administrative and legal business for the crown, particularly between 1450 and 1460. There is evidence to suggest that he was also much involved with Cornish sea rovers (72e below).

71a

C1/28/455–69 *Printed in full by Kingsford 1925, pp. 183ff.*

CHANCELLOR The bishop of Exeter

DATE 25 July 1460–15 March 1465

PETITIONER Francis Junyent, master and owner of the galley, *St. Anthony and St. Francis* of Barcelona in Catalonia in the realm of the king of Aragon, who was a long-standing friend and ally of King Edward IV and his predecessors.

COMPLAINT Merchants of Flanders and Southampton had shipped in the petitioner's galley goods valued at £12,000 or more, including goods valued at £3,000 belonging to the petitioner himself and to certain men of Aragon as specified in an attached schedule. The petitioner had brought the galley into Plymouth on 27 November 1449 to shelter from a storm. There it had been captured by armed wrongdoers, pirates and robbers in the ship, *Edward of Polruan*, and the barge, *Mackerel of Fowey*, who had ejected the petitioner, merchants and crew—disregarding the friendship between Aragon and England and letters of safe conduct sealed by Henry VI, recently called king of England—and brought it to Fowey, where they had broken into it, and divided the cargo and everything else in it at the time among the victuallers and owners of the two vessels, and others, in order to have their support for the wrongful taking and in their defence against complaints arising from it.

REQUEST In the usual terms, for writs *subpoena* to everyone named in a second schedule to appear in chancery to be examined and to abide by the chancellor's award etc. so that the petitioner might have satisfaction for the loss of the galley and goods, for which he had never had any satisfaction or restitution, and for his costs and damages.

Latin

The schedule of the goods shipped in the galley of Francis Junyent of Barcelona.

The schedule sets out:

I.   The names of thirteen men of Barcelona, with the occupations of most of them and the goods of each, the port at which they were shipped, i.e. Sluis or Southampton, and, in several cases, the names of shippers.

II.   The equipment of the galley, and the personal belongings and the merchandise of the petitioner himself.[1]

III.   The names of five men of Valencia, with their goods, the ports of shipment and, in one or two cases, the shippers.

[1]A very detailed list of valuable instruments and articles of various kinds carried by the master and owner of this luxurious galley.

71c

The schedule of the names of the pirates and robbers:

I.   Six names, including John Cornewe,[1] in the barge, *Mackerel of Fowey*.

II.   Seven names, including Thomas Philip[2] and John Attred,[2] of men in the ship, *Edward of Polruan*.

III.   The names of five victuallers of the *Mackerel*, including John Browne.[3]

IV.   The names of five victuallers of the *Edward*, including Thomas Philip and Hugh Courtney.

V.   The names of six owners of the *Edward*, including Thomas Philip and one other of the victuallers, and John Perkyn.[4]

VI.   The names of forty-seven other persons who had part of the goods, including John Colshill, knight,[5] John Arundell of Talvern,[5] William Lytilton, William White and John Stephyn.[6]

[1]Cp. 64 above.
[2]Cp. 65
[3]Cp. 59 and 64.
[4]Cp. 33
[5]Cp. 64 note.
[6]Cp. 60

71d

The answer of Robert Ferrour to Francis Junyent's bill.

Robert Ferrour, one of the 47 persons named in the schedule of those who had part of the goods, admitted that a bonnet and a pair of knives had come into his hands and said that they had been delivered to Thomas Bodulgate by virtue of a commission to him and others. He denied that he had received anything else, or had supported the pirates and wrong-doers in any way, and was ready to prove in whatever way the chancellor awarded. He prayed to be dismissed with his costs and damages etc.

71e

The answer of Thomas Butside, also named in the schedule, who admitted receiving 2 yards of woollen cloth, 3 yards of linen, 2,000 pins, 3 bonnets, 4 bundles of linen thread, all of which had been delivered to Thomas Bodulgate etc. (as in the answer of Robert Ferrour).

71f

The answer of John Mark, also named in the schedule, who admitted receiving a sword, 6 bonnets, a painted cloth, 2 barrels of red herrings, all of which, except the sword, had been delivered to Thomas Bodulgate, commissioner, on 30 February 1450, as appeared by an indenture made between them, and which John Mark was ready to produce. The sword had been delivered later to John Colshull, knight, another of the commissioners. John Mark denied that anything else had come into his hands, or that he had aided the pirates and prayed to be dismissed etc. (as in the answer of Robert Ferrour).

71g

The answer of Thomas Pennarth, also named in the schedule, who admitted that 3 yards of woollen cloth, 10 yards of holland cloth, 11 bonnets and 6 pairs of knives had been delivered to Henry More for him, he having been in London at the time, and knowing nothing of it. Lowes Scott, who had then been factor of Francis Junyent and the merchants of the galley, had arranged that Thomas Pennarth should leave London and go to Cornwall to act for them in procuring the restitution of the galley, and the goods and merchandise. Thomas Pennarth had been promised 40s. and his costs by Lowes Scott. When he arrived in Cornwall and discovered that Henry More had received goods on his behalf, he had caused them to be returned to Lowes Scott, at the command of John Arundell, one of the commissioners. He denied that anything else had come into his hands or that he had aided the pirates etc. (as in the previous answers).

71h

The answer of James Durneford, esquire, also named in the schedule, who made protestation that the bill was insufficient to require an answer in this court, and made declaration specifically denying all the charges in the bill (71a above), which denial he was ready to prove etc. (as in previous answers).

71i

The answer of Nicholas Carmynow, named in the schedule as a victualler of the barge, *Mackerel of Fowey*, which he denied. He admitted that $3\frac{1}{2}$ pieces of whole woollen cloth, $1\frac{1}{2}$ pieces of linen cloth, 40,000 pins, 30 saddler's plates, 8 bundles of saddler's wire, 18 bundles of linen thread, 3 bundles of bonnets, a large brass pan, 2 pieces of serge, 12 pairs of spurs, a latten basin and 12 pairs of scissors were delivered to his servant, Henry Benett, while he was in London, and without his knowledge, and as soon as he knew of it he caused it all to be delivered to the commissioner, Thomas Bodulgate, Lowys Scott, and Daniell Justynyan, who was attorney of all the merchants of the galley.

Nicholas Carmynow also said that he had been given 2 yards of grey woollen cloth, price 40d. the yard, 3 double bonnets, dyed a fast colour, price 8d. a bonnet, 500 Flemish pins, 6 paris balls, 12 ' grynnyngames ' price 6d., 6 pairs of spurs with short pricks and no rowels, price 12d., 10 yards of holland cloth, price 6d. a yard, 6 pairs of pencases and inkhorns, price 12d., 3 pieces of white saddler's plate, price $2\frac{1}{2}$d., 1 piece of saddler's wire, 3 fathoms long, price 2d., 1 quire of paper, price $1\frac{1}{2}$d., 2 pairs of Flemish knives, price $1\frac{1}{2}$d. the pair, 1 painted cloth, 2 yards long, of the value of 2s., 100 tack nails, price $\frac{1}{2}$d., for which goods he was ready to satisfy Francis Junyent and the merchants or their owners.

He denied that the galley, or anything else had come into his hands or that he had aided the pirates etc. (as in previous answers).

71j

The answer of Thomas Tregarthyn, named in the schedule as a victualler of the *Edward of Polruan*, which he denied. He admitted that $7\frac{1}{2}$ yards of cloth was delivered to Thomas [G . . .]n on his behalf during his absence in London, and as soon as he knew of it he had caused it to be delivered to Lowys Scott, attorney of the merchants, who had come to him in Lincoln's Inn in London and asked him to accompany him to Cornwall to help in the recovery of the goods and merchandise promising him a fee of 5 marks. They went together to Cornwall, but the goods and merchandise had been carried off 14 days before they arrived. But Thomas Tregarthyn had searched for them after his arrival, and had caused John Norton, one of the leading pirates, to be taken and brought to London, where he had been committed to the king's bench. Lowys Scott had delivered some of the goods from the galley which had been restored to him, to Thomas Tregarthyn in payment of 40s. of the 5 marks fee. And he said that nothing else had come into his hands, nor had he ever aided the pirates etc. (as before).

71k

The answer of John Watte to whom a writ of *subpoena* had been delivered, alleging that goods from the galley had come into the hands of John

Wattis, but he said that this was an error, as he was John Watte of Bodmin, tucker, and was never known as John Wattis. The man for whom the writ was intended was John Wattis, sometime of Restormel, parker. John Watte said further that none of the goods from the galley had come into his hands as he was ready to prove etc.

711

The reply of Francis Junyent to the answer of Nicholas Carmynow and others reasserting that Carmynow and Tregarthyn were victuallers of the barge as alleged in his bill; and—since neither they nor the remainder of the wrongdoers denied having had part of the merchandise in the galley for which he had received no satisfaction—he prayed that both Carmynow and Tregarthyn and the others be compelled to satisfy him in accordance with the law and statutes provided for such a case.

Editor's Note. There had been proceedings concerning the galley and its cargo soon after it was captured. Commissions dated 28 January and 18 February 1450 were issued on behalf of merchants of Catalonia and Genoa and Cologne. They imply that the ship had been restored to Francis Junyent with some of the merchandise and was being taken by him to Southampton (*CPR 1446–52* pp. 319, 320). He, with Daniel Justynyan and Lewis Scott, did, in fact, acknowledge the receipt from Nicholas Carmynow and some others named in the schedules attached to his bill (71a above) of specified, but not priced, goods so similar to those enumerated in the answer of Nicholas Carmynow (71i above) that there can be no doubt that they were part of the galley's cargo, although there seems to be an error in the date of the memorandum of the acknowledgement of the receipt as entered in the close roll. (*CCR 1447–54* pp. 169, 174. The date is given as 'March 1449 28 Henry VI.' But March 28 Henry VI was 1450, which would agree with the dates of the commissions).

72a

C1/143/73

CHANCELLOR The archbishop of Canterbury

DATE 7 March 1455–11 October 1456

PETITIONER William Joce of Bristol, merchant

COMPLAINT The petitioner had loaded a barge called the *Katherine of Bayonne*, master: William Suharra, at Bayonne[1] with wine, iron and saffron, and had sailed thence to St. Ives[2] in Cornwall, where the master cast anchor and rode in the harbour for two days. Then Pers Treunwith, James Nycholl, John Polpere, John Harry, John Petyt, Graunt John and many others of St. Ives came aboard the barge in a friendly manner, but when they had entered it, they robbed and spoiled it, carrying away the wine,

iron and saffron without any kind of authority. The petitioner had complained to the king of the wrongful taking of the goods, whereupon a
commission had been directed to certain men to inquire into the matter,
and an inquiry held by them had found that the taking had been wrongful, and which people had done it, and had returned the finding into
chancery where it remained of record. Nevertheless the petitioner was
not of sufficient influence to sue for execution, and dared not go near St.
Ives for fear that the wrongdoers would kill him. Moreover they had
associated with them misguided men of the town, such as seamen and sea
rovers of various nations,[3] and had shared the petitioner's goods with them,
so that he would be deprived of remedy for ever unless he had the chancellor's aid on his behalf. And all this had been by the instigation of two
of the wrongdoers i.e. James Nycoll and John Polpere, who were of greater
substance than the others.

REQUEST That the chancellor would therefore consider the foregoing and
grant two writs *subpoena* directed to these two men commanding them to
appear before the king in chancery on a day and under a penalty fixed by
the chancellor to answer to the foregoing as right and conscience required,
for the love of God etc.

Pledges of prosecution: Nicholas Opy, gentleman, William White, yeoman,
both of London.

[1]This may be a mistake for Bordeaux. Cp. 72c below and *CPR 1461–67* p. 201.
[2]*Seynt Ia*
[3]*as maryners and skymers of the see of dyvers nacyons*

Editor's Note. Five other records of chancery proceedings concerning complaints by William Joce, merchant of Bristol, about the capture of the
barge *Katherine* are printed in full by Kingsford with a detailed discussion
of the incident. He did not include the above petition, no doubt because
it is filed out of its chronological order, but it is clearly the earliest of the
group, none of which relate to the commission and return mentioned in it.

The printed documents follow.

72b

C1/26/403 *See Kingsford, 1925, pp. 97 ff., 197 ff.*, for this and the next four
documents.

CHANCELLOR The bishop of Winchester

DATE 11 October 1456–7 July 1460

PETITIONER William Joce of Bristol, merchant.

COMPLAINT The terms are set out of statute 27 Edward III, (1353) cap. 13
providing for the recovery by the owner, without any suit at common law,
of goods plundered at sea and brought to England.
    The petitioner—having the king's safe conduct for two ships of Bayonne
of 160 tons or less—had loaded one of them, the *Katherine of Bayonne*, with

42 tuns of wine and 10 tons of iron of his own valued at £400. On its way to England, the ship had been seized at sea by Otes Treunwith and others of St. Ives, Cornwall, brought there with its contents, taken possession of, and kept as his own by Otes to the great damage of the petitioner without the chancellor's aid.

REQUEST In the usual terms for a writ directed to Otes Treunwith ordering him to appear in chancery to be examined and judged as reason and conscience required, at the reverence of God etc.

Pledges of prosecution: John Lotesdon of Glastonbury, Somerset, Thomas Matthew of Bristol, both gentlemen.

72c

C1/27/412

CHANCELLOR George, bishop of Exeter

DATE 1461

PETITIONERS William Joce of Bristol, merchant and Richard Burton.

COMPLAINT The petitioners and Bartelot de Rever[1] had been granted letters of licence and safe conduct by Henry VI on 8 October 1451 for a ship of 160 tons, or two ships of the same tonnage or less, and the petitioners had freighted the *Katherine of Bayonne*, master: William Suharra, seaman of Bayonne, at Bordeaux, with 10 tons of iron, 17 tuns of wine, 80 lb. of saffron and 40lb. of ivory and other goods and merchandise valued at £700. The barge had left Bordeaux on 7 December 1451 for Bristol, and reached the coast near St. Ives on 24 December, and John Calmady and many other wrongdoers seized it when at anchor. The record of an inquiry before the justices showed that John Calmady had the great part of the goods.

REQUEST That the chancellor would compel John Calmady, who was present in court, to restore the goods or their value to the petitioner, with his damages in accordance with the statutes etc.

Pledges of prosecution: William Ploughright, Thomas Wall, both of London, gentlemen.

[1]*Barteley de Rever* inserted above the line. There are other signs of alteration to the document.

72d

C1/27/412B The answer of John Calmady to the bill of William Joce.

John Calmady, by protestation, denied that the barge and cargo were of the value alleged in the bill, which was insufficient to require him to answer.

He said that a safe conduct and licence had been granted to Bartelot de la Rever of Bayonne, esquire, and to Machyng de Lace, Edward Wilkok, Thomas Smalcombe and William Joce by the late king, Henry, and they had been named by Bartelot for a ship of 160 tons, or two ships of the same tonnage or less, and for 48 seamen of Bayonne or other ports there, to be freighted with specified and other merchandise and brought to England.

And that William Joce by virtue of this safe conduct had freighted two ships of San Sebastian at Bordeaux, both of which he had brought safely to England, one to Bristol and the other to Barnstaple, where he had discharged them. And that the *Katherine of Bayonne* was the *Katherine of San Vicente* of Spain and not of Bayonne; and William Joce had no safe conduct for it, except the document which had expired by use for the other two ships, and which did not give the ship's particulars; and that neither it nor any other safe conduct was in the barge at the time it was seized.

He was ready to prove all this etc. and prayed to be dismissed from the court etc.

72e

CI/27/413

CHANCELLOR The bishop of Exeter

DATE 24 March 1462–23 August 1463

PETITIONER William Joce of Bristol, merchant.

COMPLAINT As in 71c above in reference to the grant (to the petitioner only) of licence and safe conduct, the freighting of the *Katherine of Bayonne*, its departure from Bordeaux, and arrival on the coast near St. Ives on 24 December 1451. Then sets out that 14 named wrongdoers and pirates, including John Calmady (and Piers Treunwith, John Harry Barowe, Graunde John, but not the others mentioned in 72a) and others not named, captured the ship and cargo and robbed and despoiled them. After which the petitioner had come to John Arundell, then sheriff of Cornwall, and showed him the safe conduct and licence, and had them publicly read in the shire hall of Lostwithiel. Richard Penpons of Cornwall, gentleman, who was owner and victualler of part of the pinnace which had captured the barge, and had received most of the cargo, was present, and asserted that the barge, goods and merchandise had been lawfully taken, and that he would justify the capture. His influence was such that the petitioner had no hope of obtaining justice against the wrongdoers and pirates and dared not sue further for recovery of his goods and merchandise in Lostwithiel, for fear of death.

The chancellor had, however, directed a commission, dated 24 March 1462,[1] to Henry Bodrygan, esquire, and others to arrest the evildoers and pirates and bring them into chancery to answer both king and petitioner. The latter with some of the commissioners and several servants of Henry

Bodrygan were approaching St. Ives on 15 August 1462 to execute the commission when Richard Penpons heard of it and incited a crowd of 80 or more riotous people, arrayed as for war, to look for the petitioner in a house outside St. Ives. Not finding him there, they followed him and his party to Redruth, and would have killed them, had they not eluded them as was known to the shire.

REQUEST For an order to a sergeant-at-arms or a *subpoena* to bring Richard Penpons into the court of chancery since it had been by his maintenance that the petitioner had lost his goods, and when he appeared to charge him under a sufficiently large penalty not to depart from the court until he had either answered and satisfied the petitioner or found sureties to do so, and to do and receive what the court should award and as law and conscience required, for the love of God etc.

Pledges of prosecution: Andrew James of Southampton, merchant; Thomas Routhe of the town of Westminster in Middlesex, gentleman.

[1]*CPR 1461–67* pp. 68, 201

72f

C1/27/413B

The replication of William Joce of Bristol, merchant, against the answer[1] of Richard Penpons.

William Joce said, by protestation, that the answer was insufficient in law to require him to answer. He said that the *Katherine* was a ship of Bayonne and not of San Vicente when he freighted it by virtue of the safe conduct and licence, which had been granted in the way described in his bill of complaint, and which was in the ship when it was despoiled.

He also said that—since Richard Penpons did not deny that he had incited the riot against the king's commission, nor the despoiling of the *Katherine*, nor that he was victualler and owner of the pinnace of St. Ives and had received part of the goods—he sought that Richard Penpons be compelled to make restitution according to the laws and statutes provided for such a case.

He also said that although neither the ship's name nor the names of the master or owner appeared in the safe conduct and licence, nevertheless they were valid. Moreover, he said that Richard Penpons had received most of the captured goods; and he denied that he had brought the two ships of San Sebastian into Bristol and Barnstaple under the same safe conduct and licence, as was alleged in the answer. All of which he was ready to prove etc.

[1]Richard Penpons'answer has not survived.

Editor's Note. The correctness of the particulars of the safe conduct and licence given by John Calmady in his answer (72d) are confirmed by its exemplification, which was entered on the patent roll on 14 January 1452, at the request of Otto Berowe (*CPR 1446–52* p. 530). It was also true that a ship came to Bristol with this safe conduct, since it is the first of a large number of such documents entered in the *Great Red Book of Bristol*. The names of the master (who was not William Suharra) and the crew appear in the margin of the entry, but the name of the ship was not given. (Veale, Text I, pp. 181 ff.). Some years earlier, statute 15 Hen. VI. cap. III had provided that a safe conduct must contain the name of the ship as well as those of the master and owner, and this, with only one or two exceptions, was complied with in the documents entered subsequently in the *Great Red Book*.

73

C1/28/476 *Many words illegible*

CHANCELLOR George, bishop of Exeter

DATE 25 July 1460–23 August 1463

PETITIONERS John Stokker the younger, and William Stokker, both of London, merchants.

COMPLAINT The petitioners had loaded and freighted a hulk called the *Christopher of Bergen op Zoom*,[1] master: Mathew Johnson, at the Bay in Brittany, with various merchandise of theirs, i.e.: 117 'chares'[2] of salt, 300 [. . .] of 'vittry'[3] and [. . .] dozen of lampreys, to be taken from the Bay to the port of London. The ship sailed from the Bay towards London and was on the high sea on the coast of Brittany, near the Race of Founteney, on 27 January 1460 when a carvel called the *Peter Courteney*, of which Hugh Courteney, knight, had then been and still was owner and victualler, [having? carvel master?] and well armed men, arrayed for war, assaulted the hulk, and entered it, and took and carried away the [cargo? which came into the?] possession of Hugh Courteney, to the petitioners' great hurt and damage of 500 marks.

REQUEST That the chancellor would consider the foregoing and cause a writ of *subpoena* to be directed to Hugh Courteney commanding him to appear on a given day and place to answer in the matter, and [compel him to compensate] the petitioners as conscience required, or else to keep him in prison; for which the petitioners would continually pray for the chancellor.

[1] *Barowe uppon Zoon*
[2] ?Char = a weight of lead. *O.E.D.*
[3] ?Vitry = a kind of canvas.

74

C1/30/60 *Damaged*

CHANCELLOR Master Robert Kirkeham, keeper of the king's great seal and the rolls of chancery.

DATE 23 August 1463–25 October 1463

PETITIONERS John Jay, John Hawkes, John Magwyn and Gilbert[1] Smyth of the town of Bristol, merchants.

COMPLAINT Four years previously the petitioners had loaded a ship [called the *Marie of Dordrecht* at] Bordeaux with 220 tuns of Gascony wine and 30 pipes of woad and other merchandise valued at 3,000 marks, and on the way home the ship, wine and woad and all other merchandise [had been seized] robbed and despoiled at sea by Hugh Courteney, knight, and his adherents. The petitioners had not obtained restitution for any part of the robbery [although they had sued] in chancery and were still doing so. The 30 pipes of woad had been brought to Topsham in Devonshire and were in the keeping of the bailiff of that town and [. . .] and decreased to the great hurt of the petitioners.

REQUEST That Master Robert Kirkeham would consider the foregoing and to address a writ to the bailiffs of Topsham [ordering them] under a heavy penalty to keep the woad safely without diminution or deliverance of any of it to anyone until they had received other command from the chancery under the king's great seal, at the reverence of God and in way of justice.

[1]*Gybon*

Editor's Note. Two commissions appear on the patent roll for 1460 relating to the capture of the *Marie of Dordrecht*,—whose master was given as Herman Taillour—by pirates in Sir Hugh Courteneys' *Peter Courteney* together with *le Galyot*, owned by John Fenell, chaplain, Thomas Adam and John Mellys. The first, dated 27 February, named the complainants as the four who later presented the above petition (the date of which in 1463 is fixed by the name of the chancellor) and eleven other merchants of Bristol, and stated that the cargo had consisted of 240 tuns of wine, 60 pipes of woad, and also 10 tons of iron and 200 lbs. of saffron; and that the ship had been taken on its way to Bristol: the three commissioners were to hold inquiries in Cornwall as to the identity of the captors, and of those into whose hands the ship and cargo had come, and to make restitution of the latter or their value, imprisoning both those who refused and the captors.

The second, dated 20 October, and directed to nine commissioners, Richard Penpons among them, not only gave the four petitioners above as complainants but also 39 merchants of Bristol, including eight of the eleven named in February. The ship was called *le Marie of Danzig*, *alias of Dordrecht*, and capture was said to have taken place at Scilly, and the captors to have been Englishmen in the same two ships, equipped for war, who had brought their prize to Fowey and disposed of it, to the value of

£2,713 13s. 4d. among themselves and the owners and victuallers, throughout Cornwall and Devon. The commissioners were again instructed to make inquiries in those counties as to who were the captors and into whose hands the ship and its equipment and cargo had come, to imprison the guilty and cause restitution to be made (*CPR 1452–61* pp. 612, 619).

The discrepancies between the complaints recited in the commissions and that of John Jay and his three fellow petitioners with regard to the amount of the cargo, can be accounted for by the large number of complainants in the former, with whose property the four petitioners would not be concerned. The latter's complaint suggests that at least some of the goods had been tracked down.

No further record of the proceedings has been found, but an order to produce Hugh Courteney, knight, in chancery, under a penalty of £2,000, was issued on 8 February 1463, since he had failed to answer to a writ, the cause, however, was not disclosed. He had been one among many commissioned in the previous year to take ships and crews, and to induce the inhabitants of various hundreds in Cornwall to victual them, for the king's fleet against his enemies (*CCR 1461–68* p. 158 *CPR 1461–67* p. 204).

75a

C1/27/262 *This and the two documents following are printed in full by Kingsford op. cit. pp. 200 ff.*

CHANCELLOR The bishop of Exeter

DATE 25 July 1460–17 May 1462

PETITIONERS John Poke, Rauf Moton, and Thomas Payn, merchants of Bristol.

COMPLAINT The petitioners, with a licence and safe conduct granted by Henry, lately king of England, had freighted the ship, *Marie of Biscay* in Spain, at Bordeaux, and loaded it with 57 tuns of Gascon wine and iron, saffron, lampreys, coats of mail and helmets, valued at £439. On its way to Bristol it was captured on the high sea by John Michell of Bodinnick and John Gravell, seaman of Golants,[1] with many other pirates and robbers in two carvels—the *Carvel of Tuke* and the *Mighell of Fowey*—on 22 April 1460, and taken to Fowey on 1 May. There Thomas Bodulgate had encouraged and commanded the captors to plunder the ship of its cargo, which remained in his hands. The petitioners had been ready to prove their ownership of the goods, but had been unable to obtain restitution.

REQUEST That the chancellor would compel Thomas Bodulgate—then present in court—to make restitution of all the goods and merchandise to the petitioners in accordance with the laws and statutes etc., and they would specially pray to God for him.

[1]*Golenance*

75b

LETTERS TESTIMONIAL: To let all Christian people who saw or heard these letters know that the *Marie of Biscay* had been freighted with Gascon wine etc. (*as set out above*) and was captured at sea (*as above*) and brought to Fowey on 1 May 1460: and that the signatories to the letters testified that the wine, saffron, iron and other merchandise in the ship as well as its gear and other goods in cabins and coffers had been plundered by Thomas Bodulgate, esquire, and divided among himself and others as he pleased, contrary to conscience and right and to the safe conduct and licence. They also testified that Thomas Bodulgate had taken 4 tuns of the wine to his own house and had set aside 10 tuns of it to maintain a plea against its owners, the merchants of Bristol, and distributed all the rest of the cargo among the owners and crews of the carvels, who would have restored the whole of it to the Bristol owners but for Bodulgate's influence.

The names of Harry Bodrugan and twenty three other ' inhabitants about the water of Fowey,' who had sealed the letters on 28 September 1461 follow.

75c

This is a copy of 75a above endorsed with a memorandum that the bill and the answer, deposition, examination, commission, inquiry and letters testimonial attached to it[1] had been read in the court of chancery before the bishop of Exeter, the chief justices of the two benches, the king's sergeants, the king's attorneys and others, and that judgement was given on 17 May, that the complainants might recover £300 against Thomas Bodulgate for part of the goods, and sue for the rest of them against those who were in possession of them.

[1] The letters testimonial only have survived.

76

C1/30/40

CHANCELLOR Robert Kirkeham, keeper of the king's great seal and master of the rolls of his chancery.

DATE 23 August–25 October 1463 (or perhaps 10 April to 14 May 1464)

PETITIONER Henry Vaghan, merchant of Bristol.

COMPLAINT The petitioner had recently shipped by virtue of the king's licence under the great seal, 36 whole cloths, 32 dozens of ' straits out of grain '[1] and 20 cloths of welsh frieze in a Spanish ship called the *Mary of Guipuscoa*[2] of 100 tons, the master of which, under God, was Ochoa Daromaye and which had been in Bristol under the king's safe conduct. The petitioner had fully paid the king's officers all the customs and tolls due on the cloth as the cocket, made and delivered under the seal of the Bristol customs, showed. After which the ship with the goods, having sailed out of the port of Bristol, was driven by contrary winds into the port of Ilfracombe in Devonshire, where they were arrested by Lord FitzWareyn and his officers, without any reasonable cause, and detained. The petitioner had immediately and many times requested Lord FitzWareyn and his officers to restore the cloths to him as right and conscience required, but they were absolutely refusing to do so, to the great damage of the petitioner.

REQUEST That Robert Kirkeham, having carefully considered the foregoing, would show justice by addressing a writ to Lord FitzWareyn strictly ordering the delivery of the cloths to the petitioner or his attorney in accordance with good faith and conscience, and he would pray heartily to God for him.

¹The opposite of broad cloth, without the expensive dye, grain.
²*Ipusco*

Editor's Note. The *Mary of Guipuscoa* called at Bristol under a safe conduct naming the master as either Johannes de Fontarabia or Ochoa Daramayo, and dated 16 September 1462 for one year. A licence to trade was issued to William Joce and Henry Vaghan, merchants of Bristol, on 9 August 1463 permitting them or their agents to go, once or more often during the following year, to France, Brittany, or Spain to buy goods and merchandise, to load them in any ship they pleased and return to England to sell them. (Veale, Text Part II, pp. 102, 108). If these were the documents referred to in the complaint above, their dates suggest that the safe conduct might have been out of date by the time the ship was arrested in Ilfracombe.

William Bourchier of Fitzwarren was employed on commissions concerning shipping in the west country after the accession of Edward IV, including one in May 1462 to arrest John Michell of Bodinnick and others and bring them before the king in chancery. (*CPR 1461–67* pp. 34, 37, 202, 204, 232, and 75a above).

77

C1/32/74

CHANCELLOR The archbishop of York

DATE 15 March 1465–8 June 1467

PETITIONER Ralph Mercer of Dartmouth, seaman, master of the *Nicholas of the Tower.*

COMPLAINT The petitioner had recently arrested in Yarmouth harbour a ship called a crayer, freighted with Dutch ware and stuff valued at 100 marks, which was forfeit to the king in accordance with the proclamation of the act providing for this. Afterwards Christopher Bootle, merchant, and John Gille, both of York, and others had carried away the crayer, which, because of the forfeiture, was to the king's great loss; and John Gille and the others had now maliciously begun false actions of trespass and detinue against the petitioner and had him arrested and imprisoned in the city of York, intending to cause him great damage for his rightful action of arresting the crayer and Dutch ware, contrary to all right and conscience.

REQUEST That the chancellor would grant a *corpus cum causa* directed to the mayor and sheriffs of York, and to each of them, to be returned on a day fixed by him, and with a penalty, taking into account that the matter concerned the king's interest, as well as the relief and release of the petitioner, who would pray for the preservation of the chancellor's noble estate.

Editor's Note. It had been enacted in parliament that, after 2 February 1464, no merchant, native or alien should import merchandise from Holland, Zeeland and Flanders or any other territory then held by the Duke of Burgundy or sell them under penalty of forfeiture (Rot. Part. V. p. 565a *CPR 1461–67* p. 517). Ralph Mercer was accused with others of Dartmouth in 1467 of seizing goods from ships of Burgandy (below 79).

78

C1/32/75

CHANCELLOR The archbishop of York

DATE 15 March 1465–8 June 1467

PETITIONER Martyn de Sarras, merchant of Guyenne.

COMPLAINT About four years earlier John Cop', Thomas Wyer and William Howler, merchants of Barnstaple, had bargained with the petitioner and delivered to him as many cloths called straits[1] as equalled the value of 30 tons of iron or thereabouts, which he was to send to the three merchants in England at their risk in whatever ship or ships he could find. He had shipped all the iron to them at various times as he had been able to find shipping, and all of it had come into their hands except 7 tons and a pipe, which had been taken into Brittany as the goods of Englishmen[2] about three years previously. Although the petitioner had often been at Barnstaple since and in company with the three merchants, they had never questioned him about 7 tons and 1 pipe until recently, when they had seen that a vessel of his, with various merchandise, had come into Barnstaple whereupon they had attached various goods of his, i.e. 5 tons and 1 pipe of iron, 4 rolls of bever, and 6s. 8d., and were keeping them under arrest although he had offered before the mayor of Barnstaple that he would pay them every penny of their damage if they would swear that they had not agreed to take the whole risk of the 30 tons of iron.[3] This they absolutely refused to do, but would have the petitioner's goods which they had attached by might against right and conscience.

REQUEST That the chancellor would consider the foregoing and grant a *certiorari*, directed to the mayor to have the matter examined before him in chancery, whereupon the petitioner would specially pray to God for his noble estate.

[1]Cp. above 76 footnote 1.
[2]i.e. enemy goods
[3]*that they should not stand to all the adventure of the said XXX tonnes of iren*

Editor's Note. The petitioner had complained in 1461 of the capture by pirates of a ship of Guyenne which he and another man had brought to London under safe conduct loaded with wine, and reloaded with cloth and other merchandise. It had been seized on the return journey and taken to Sandwich (*CPR 1461–67* p. 65).

79

C1/33/179

CHANCELLOR The archbishop of York

DATE 1467

PETITIONER John de Verre, subject of the duke of Burgundy, for himself and his companions.[1]

COMPLAINT The king, at the request of the duke of Burgundy, had graciously granted judgement and definitive sentence according to truth, equity and good conscience to the petitioner and his companions against John Rawlyn of Dartmouth, Walter Cok, Ralph[2] Mercer, Sir Philip Courteney, knight, John Wynart, esquire, Sir John Gardener, priest, Richard Cette, Aleyn Baker, Thomas Payne, Hugh David, Thomas Lerrent, William Robert, William Mercer, Richard Baker, Robert Mercer, William Clement, William William, Henry Coke, Thomkyn Hunt, Thomas Symond, Christopher Wynard, William Stephen, Thomas Taylowe, master, partners and victuallers of certain ships of Dartmouth, for certain goods and merchandise of the petitioners and his companions forcibly taken on the sea by John Rawlyn, Walter Cok, Ralph Mercer, and their confederacy contrary to right and to the long established truce and commercial intercourse between the king, his subjects and realm, and the duke, his subjects and country, as was more fully set out in the sentence.

REQUEST That the chancellor would consider the foregoing carefully and advise the king that the sentence should be executed and justice done immediately, and that John Rawlyn, Walter Cok, Ralph Mercer and their confederacy should make restitution and give satisfaction by payment without delay for the goods and merchandise in accordance with justice and at reverence of God etc.

[1]*consortes*
[2]Rawlynne

Editor's Note. This petition must have been presented before 8 June 1467, when the chancellorship changed hands. It resulted, according to the patent rolls, in the appointment of commissioners on 22 December 1467 to arrest John Rawlyn (called Rawlegh) of Dartmouth, Walter Cok and Ralph Mercer in Devon and Cornwall, and to bring them before the king and council. A second commission—dated 28 November 1468—ordered the arrest and production before the council of all the men named in the petition, and also an inquiry to find who was in possession of goods and merchandise from six ships of Flanders, and what their value was. Both these commissions referred to an earlier appointment to examine the complaint of John de Verre (spelt Veer) of Zeeland and another man—a burgess of Flanders—on behalf of themselves and other part owners, victuallers and masters of the six ships. This had clearly preceded the petition. It had produced the information that the ships had been seized by John Rawlyn and his fellows, contrary to the truce with Philip, late duke of Burgundy, and plundered of wine and other merchandise and equipment valued at 4,330 crowns. After considering this finding, the king and council had given judgement that restitution should be made, but this had not been carried out. (*CPR 1467-77* p. 57, 128).

John de Verre had obtained similar chancery action some months earlier concerning a ship of his which was alleged to have been plundered, contrary to the friendship between the king and the men of Zeeland, by another Dartmouth ship, which was in the port of Kingston on Hull when its arrest and that of its owner were ordered. (Ibid. p. 29).

80

C1/33/329

CHANCELLOR The archbishop of York

DATE 15 March 1465–8 June 1467

PETITIONER Juband Huet, merchant of Gascony

COMPLAINT John Clerk, merchant, lately of Dartmouth, now living in New Salisbury,[1] owed the petitioner £115 sterling for wines which he had sold to him, as was shown by two obligations, for the sum of £125, payable 6 months previously, of which one, for £78, had been made in Bordeaux, and the other, for £46 4s. 4d. had been made in this country. The petitioner had no remedy at common law for the non payment of the £115 because he was not under its jurisdiction since he owed allegiance to another prince.

REQUEST That the chancellor would consider the foregoing carefully and grant a writ *subpoena* directed to John Clerk commanding him to appear in chancery by a certain day and under a penalty to be fixed by him, and then ordain that the petitioner should be paid the £115, in accordance with right, reason and good conscience for the love of God etc. and he would especially pray for the chancellor's noble estate.

[1] *Newe Salesbury*

Editor's Note. John Clerk of New Sarum, merchant, owned a considerable amount of property in Dartmouth and elsewhere in Devon and Somerset and in New Sarum in 1467. He seems also to have had goods and chattels in that town and elsewhere in England, and upon the sea and overseas. (*CCR 1461–68* p. 403). There is nothing to show whether he paid the debt claimed by Juband Huet whose country had ceased to be under English rule by 1453; as an alien he could not, according to a fifteenth century ruling, bring an action at common law (Pollock and Maitland, 1898 I pp. 465–6).

81

C1/36/109

CHANCELLOR The archbishop of York

DATE 15 May 1465–8 June 1467

PETITIONERS William Brewer and William Dawe

COMPLAINT The petitioners had been the owners of a ship called the *Davy of Fowey*, and while in possession of it, they had given it with all its tackle to John Treyouran and his heirs and executors for ever to the use of themselves,[1] and had put him in possession of the ship by virtue of the gift and trusting to his good faith. They had since many times asked him to return the ship and all its tackle but he had always refused to do so and still refused and had continuously occupied it and taken the profits from it and converted them to his own use, to the petitioners' great loss and damage.

REQUEST That the chancellor would consider the foregoing and that the petitioners had no remedy at common law by which they could recover the ship, and grant them a writ directed to John Treyouran to appear before the king in chancery on a day and under a penalty given by the chancellor to answer concerning the foregoing[2] and to accept what good law and conscience required, and they would pray for the chancellor's preservation.

Pledges of prosecution: John Penlyn, gentleman, Thomas Norman, yeoman, both of London.

Latin
   Endorsed: Before the king in chancery one month after the next Michaelmas day.

   [1]*to the use and behoveth of your said oratours*
   [2]*to answer doo take and receyve uppon the premyses*

Editor's Note. William Dawe had been the master of a carvel of Fowey accused with another one in 1456 of having seized the ship of a merchant of Rouen when it was under safe conduct. In December 1472 he was one of five victuallers and owners of another ship of Fowey alleged to have plundered a Spanish ship (*CPR 1452–61* p. 309 Ibid. *1467–77* p. 378).

82

C1/44/151 *Many words illegible*

CHANCELLOR Robert, bishop of Bath and Wells

DATE 23 May 1469–9 October 1470

PETITIONER David, abbot of Cleave, ' your chaplain '.

COMPLAINT King Henry III had granted the right of wreck of the sea by
letters patent to [. . .] of Cleeve[1] predecessor of the petitioner and
his successors in all their demesne lands and tenements in Poughill[2]
and Treglasten in Cornwall for ever as the letters patent—allowed before
the justices in eyre and confirmed by the present king—show more plainly;
and the petitioner and his predecessors had been in possession of the right
in all their demesne lands in the towns of Poughill and Treglasten ever
since. Recently goods coming as wreck into the petitioner's lands in
Poughill had been arrested and seized by some of his servants and tenants
on his behalf; whereupon John May of Bristol, merchant, who had been
owner of a ship called the *Raphael of Bristol*, loaded with goods and
merchandise at Danzig in Prussia, bound for Bristol and lost at sea, had
presented a petition to the chancellor asking for a commission to Lord
FitzWareyn and others to inquire whether the ship and cargo were wreck,
asserting that some of the merchants and seamen had reached land in
various ports in England and that the ship had perished at Bude Bay[3] in
Cornwall whereas it had been destroyed on the high sea. A commission
had been granted and an inquiry held by three of the commissioners:
Philip Beaumont,[4] esquire, sheriff of Devonshire, John Orchard and Walter Geynecote who had found that [some of the people] in the ship had
landed at Sandwich in Kent and others at Plymouth and that the ship
had afterwards been destroyed at Bude Bay [and that some of the?] goods
in it had come into the hands of the petitioner's servants and tenants, but
the inquiry did not find whether the ship and goods were wreck or not nor
anything more. The petitioner believed that this verdict did not exclude
him from his claim to the goods as wreck. Nevertheless the commissioners
had returned and certified falsely that Richard Harlok and Thomas
Donne and other seamen who had been in the ship when it was destroyed
had come ashore at Bude Bay, which was not true as the petitioner was
ready to prove before the chancellor by the grace of God.

As a result of the return and certification and at the special suit and
petition of John May, a commission had been directed to Humphrey, earl
of Devonshire, and other [. . . to cause?] restitution [to be made] of all
the goods which had been found to be in the hands of the petitioner's
servants and to imprison any of them who refused until it had been done,
and to inquire into the whereabouts and make restitution of the remainder
of the merchandise. On the strength of this, the commissioners were
proposing to compel the petitioner's servants to give up the goods, which
he believed to be contrary to right and conscience, having regard both to
his right to the wreck and to the falsity of the return and certificate concerning which the chancellor had not been notified.

REQUEST That the chancellor would consider the foregoing, and how, if the goods should be [taken out?] of the hands [of the petitioner's servants?] he would never be able to recover them although he understood that he had true right and title to them, and grant a writ to Humphrey, earl of Devonshire and the other commissioners to cease to execute the commission until further order, and a writ *subpoena* directed [to John May] to appear in chancery on a given day to answer, show and set forth[5] such evidence as he had of his interest and [to submit to whatever judgement] the chancellor thought reasonable; for the love of God etc.

Pledges of prosecution: John Hopping of London, gentleman, Thomas C[. . .]an of Cleyve in Devonshire, yeoman.

[1]*Clyve*
[2]*Poghwell*
[3]*Bedebay*
[4]*Bemond*
[5]*aley*

Editor's Note. A charter of grant by Hubert de Burgh to the monks of Cleeve of his land of Treglasten and 'Pochewell' was entered on the patent roll for 1227. There was no specific reference to the right of wreck but the grant included all appurtenances (*CPR 1225–32* p. 165).

The two commissions referred to by the petitioner were dated 20 April 1468 and 22 May 1469. They gave in more detail the facts about the loss of the *Raphael* as set out in the petition. The inquiry had been held in Barnstaple on 25 August 1468 and found that the ship had disembarked merchants and seamen at Grimsby, Holderness and Hull as well as Sandwich and then, on its way to Bristol, had been forced by storm into Bude Bay in the river Severn where it had dragged its anchors and been driven ashore near Kilkhampton in November 1467. It was also found that John May had been on land waiting for the ship and that other seamen as well as Richard Harlok and Thomas Donne had been on it when it was wrecked and had survived. Details were given of the cargo and gear, valued at £1,000, part of which had come into the hands of three named men, who refused to return it, and the rest had been cast ashore and carried away by others although it was not wreck. The commissioners had been ordered to cause restitution and inquiry to be made as the abbot, who was not mentioned in John May's complaints, stated in his petition.

83

C1/44/212

CHANCELLOR The bishop of Bath and Wells

DATE 14 April 1471–20 September 1472

PETITIONER John Walker of the town of Southampton, merchant.

COMPLAINT Recently, i.e. on 11 November 1470, the petitioner had been the owner of some sweet wines i.e. 6 tuns of bastard, 3½ tuns of sweet wine called 'wine cute', and 21 tuns of Romney, valued at £251, in a ship called the *Mary of Gruyn* which was lying at sea in the port of Dartmouth in Devonshire, when John Fyssher of Dartmouth with other unknown wrongdoers came and entered the ship with force and arms and carried the wine away, robbing and despoiling the petitioner of it. On the following 15 November at Dartmouth, 6 tuns of Romney valued at £18 and 1 tun of 'wine cute' valued at £10 13s. 4d. came into the hands of Richard Geffrey of Exeter, 2 tuns of Romney valued at £16 into the hands of Robert Smyth of Exeter, merchant, 2 tuns of Romney valued at £16 into the hands of Richard Unday of Exeter, 3 tuns of Romney valued at £24 into the hands of John Ken of Lyme, and 3 tuns of Romney valued at £23 into the hands of John Davy of Lyme, baker. The petitioner had not been able to obtain restitution of any of these wines.

REQUEST That the chancellor would consider the foregoing carefully and grant writs of *subpoena* out of the king's chancery addressed to each of the above named men commanding them to appear before the king in chancery under a penalty and at a time specified in the writs by the chancellor and there to abide[1] what faith and conscience required, and that the petitioner might recover his goods in accordance with the statutes provided for such a case, and he would pray to God for the chancellor.

Pledges of prosecution: William Weston, gentleman, and John Nicholas, yeoman, both of London.

[1] *to do ard resceyre*

Editor's Note. John Walker of Southampton was appointed as gauger in the port in February 1484, and granted an annuity from the customs there and in adjacent places in March (*CPR 1476–85* pp. 404, 431). A gift of all his goods, chattels and debts in England and overseas was made by him in Southampton to Richard, duke of Gloucester, William, earl of Arundel and two others in 1477 (*CCR 1476–1485* No. 473).

84

Ci/49/18

CHANCELLOR The earl of Essex, keeper of the king's great seal

DATE 23 June–17 July 1473

PETITIONER John Sonelly of Seint Brieuc[1] in Brittany

COMPLAINT The petitioner had come to Plymouth in the realm of England in September 1469, trusting to the peace and friendship between the king and the duke of Brittany, with certain goods and merchandise to offer for sale in the kingdom; and at that time and place John Cok and Thomas Wotton of Bodmin, Cornwall, mercers, had come and then and there accused the petitioner of having been in a ship of Brittany at an earlier date, specified by them, and taken certain goods and merchandise of theirs and others. Whereupon they had put him in prison where he had been detained for 7 months contrary to the peace and friendship and to all right and conscience; for it was well known, both in Plymouth and in Seint Brieuc in Brittany that he had been in Seint Brieuc at the time and on the day when they said that their goods had been taken, as appeared more clearly and of record in a letter testimonial made, after examination, under the seal of the duke of Brittany and in the possession of the petitioner. Nevertheless they had kept his goods and merchandise ever since. They had also made him find sufficient security in Plymouth for £1,000 before releasing him from prison, and this could not be discharged nor could his goods and merchandise be released to his great sorrow and utter undoing without the earl's goodwill in this behalf.

REQUEST That he would consider the foregoing and grant a writ *subpoena* directed to John Cok and Thomas Wotton strictly commanding each of them to appear before the king in chancery with a day and a penalty fixed by the earl, to be examined on the foregoing and to abide what right and conscience required, at the reverence of God etc and the petitioner would always pray for the earl's preservation.

Latin
    Endorsed: Before the king in chancery on the octave of St. Michael.

    ¹*Seint Break*

85

C1/48/432

CHANCELLOR The bishop of Durham

DATE 27 July 1473–25 February 1475

PETITIONER Nicholas Wade

COMPLAINT John Toker of Great Totnes in Devonshire, John Swete, Mochill' Saverey, John Colaton, and John Pyrs had been owners with the petitioner of a ship called the *Trinity* which had been arrested at Land-regare in Brittany. He and they had come to an agreement in Devonshire that he should pay for bringing the ship's seamen home, and that he should go to Brittany to obtain delivery of the ship, and John Toker and the others each promised him to pay their share of whatever costs, expenditure and expenses he had to lay out for the release of the ship and the return of the seamen. Whereupon the petitioner had paid for the crew's return and had gone to Brittany and had delivery of the ship, and John Toker's share of the sum which he had laid out in the matter had come to 4 marks. He had demanded payment of this amount many times from John Toker, who had refused it and was still doing so. The petitioner had no remedy at common law.

REQUEST That the chancellor would consider the foregoing carefully and grant him a writ of *subpoena* against John Toker to cause him to appear before the king in chancery at a day and time assigned by the chancellor, for the love of God etc.

Pledges of prosecution: John Hoper and John Harvey ,both yeomen of London.

Latin
    Endorsed: Before the king in chancery a month after Easter.

86

C1/48/196

CHANCELLOR Laurence, bishop of Durham

DATE 27 July 1473–25 February 1475

PETITIONER John Mercer, foreign merchant of Brittany

COMPLAINT Two years earlier or more, John Broke of Plymouth had freighted a ship of the petitioner's in Brittany with wines and other goods and merchandise saying that they were his own property. The petitioner came to Plymouth with the ship and cargo, and delivered all the wines, goods and merchandise to John Broke—who had satisfied him for his labour and for the freight of the ship—and returned to his own country. He had now come back to England to sue for the recovery of another ship which had been captured and spoiled at sea by evil disposed men of Fowey and Dartmouth contrary to the truce between King Edward IV and his cousin, the duke of Brittany; and William Mathews, tailor, of London, whom the petitioner had never known nor dealt with, had brought an action of account for 100 marks against him before the sheriffs in London, and had him arrested, alleging that he had had wines and other goods valued at 100 marks in the ship which John Broke had freighted in Brittany; and he had caused a jury to be summoned, intending to have the petitioner condemned in the action since he was a foreigner and had few acquaintances in the city and could not wage his law in this action, to his permanent impoverishment and undoing contrary to right and good conscience unless the chancellor shewed him his goodwill.

REQUEST That he would consider the foregoing and that the petitioner had never received any goods from William Mathews nor from anyone on his behalf, and grant a *corpus cum causa* directed to the sheriffs of London commanding them to bring the petitioner with the causes of his arrest before the king in chancery on a day fixed by the chancellor to be examined in the foregoing and to do further whatever seemed to the court to be in accordance with right and good conscience, for the love of God etc.

Latin
    Endorsed: Before the king Wednesday i.e. 27 October.

87

C1/59/95

CHANCELLOR The bishop of Lincoln

DATE 28 September 1475–3 September 1480

PETITIONER John Bereman of Topsham, county Devonshire

COMPLAINT One, Stephen Freende, out of malice only and without any cause of action, had alleged false information of certain offences supposed to have been done upon the sea by the petitioner intending to vex and hinder him, and had caused him to be called before the judge of the admiralty at Horton Key, where he was being vexed and troubled and put to great expense. In fact the alleged matters had been done on land within the body of the shire not on the sea as could be sufficiently shown and so ought to be determined by the common law of the land; and the judge and clerks of the court being aware that the petitioner intended to apply for a *supersedeas* on the case, would neither charge him in writing[1] nor give him any copy on which he could sue for his remedy or make an answer and he was likely to be condemned for the supposed offences and to pay large sums of money, in great derogation of the common law and to his utter undoing, for which he had no remedy except through the chancellor.

REQUEST That the chancellor would consider the foregoing carefully and grant a *subpoena* directed to Stephen Freende commanding him to appear before the king in chancery on a day and under a penalty fixed by the chancellor to answer the foregoing as right and conscience required, for the love of God etc.

Pledges of prosecution: John Bouring, and Thomas More both of London, yeomen.

Latin
    Endorsed: Before the king in his chancery: fifteen days after St. Hilary next.

    [1] *lybell against hym in writing*

Editor's Note. In 1467 the court of the admiral of England, Ireland and Aquitaine was held at Horton Key in Southwark in a high hall by the tideway in the parish of St. Olave. This was its accustomed place in 1470 and—called Orton Key—in the next century (*CPR 1467-77* pp. 52, 184, 201. Marsden 1892 I p.lxxix).

88

C1/67/172

CHANCELLOR The bishop of Lincoln

DATE 28 September 1475–3 September 1480

PETITIONERS George Depe, John Fraunceys, William Oriall', Bernard Gelowe, and John Haket merchants of St. Malo in Brittany.

COMPLAINT The petitioners lately came sailing across the sea in a ship of St. Malo loaded with goods and merchandise, valued at £1000 and more, to the port of Poole; and as they entered the port a ship of war of Fowey, master: Jermyn Skehard, accompanied by a ship of Plymouth called the *Jesus*, loaded with wood[1]—John Sherve, William Lukas and William Smyth owners, victuallers and masters—had made war on their ship and taken it with great force and put the men ashore at Poole. The Breton ship itself was led away westward by the ship of Fowey, contrary to the truce and friendship between the king and the duke of Brittany. And it happened that the mast of the ship of Plymouth had been broken by a storm at sea and the ship was driven to Hamble[2] at the Rise, which port was under the jurisdiction of the mayor of Southampton. He, having information of the event, sent various people there to arrest William Lukas and the ship. William Lukas was under security at Southampton but was likely to be carried off by the contrivance of seamen,[3] to the petitioner's utter undoing without the chancellor's goodwill on this behalf.

REQUEST The grant, in consideration of the foregoing, of a *corpus cum causa* directed to the mayor and bailiffs of Southampton to bring up William Lukas before the king in chancery at a day fixed by the chancellor; and for the chancellor to pronounce on the matter in accordance with reason and conscience, for the love of God etc.

Endorsed: Before the king in chancery in the octave of Michaelmas.

[1]*wode*
[2]*Hamele*
[3]*purloyned away by dyverse meanes and favour of maryners*

89a

C1/51/153 *Damaged*

CHANCELLOR The bishop of Lincoln

DATE 25 February 1475–24 June 1477

PETITIONER Harry Denys of London, grocer

COMPLAINT Mathew Andrewe of Topsham[1] in Devonshire, merchant, had bargained and fully agreed with the petitioner there on 1 August [...] 1474 that he would convey his ship, the *James of Ottermouth*, from Topsham to London in as short a time as wind and weather [allowed, and that he would] purchase and obtain an adequate safe conduct from the king of France or his admiral by the time the ship had reached London, to protect it and its merchandise, merchants and seamen from the French on the sea from the port of London to the town of Topsham, and that it would provide protection for the ship and its contents for as long as they were at sea on the voyage. He had also agreed with the petitioner that the latter should freight the ship with whatever merchandise he pleased to be conveyed from London to Topsham for which the petitioner had agreed to pay the sum of £9 of lawful money when the goods, shipped in London, had reached Topsham and been delivered to him or his deputy.

Mathew Andrewe had sent the ship to London and had also sent a message to the petitioner saying that it had arrived and that the safe conduct was there in accordance with the agreement, and, believing that the safe conduct was adequate, the petitioner had shipped madder and woad valued at £140. The ship had then sailed with the goods out of the port of London towards Topsham and had been taken on the high sea by Frenchmen because Mathew had not obtained or purchased a safe conduct as he had agreed to do; and, although the ship and goods had been lost through his deception, he did not intend to compensate or satisfy the petitioner for the loss of his goods, contrary to all right and conscience, for which the petitioner had no remedy at common law.

REQUEST That the chancellor would consider the foregoing carefully and direct a writ *subpoena* to Mathew Andrewe commanding him to appear before the king in chancery on a day and under a penalty given by the chancellor so that, upon examination before him of the foregoing, a just decision may be made[2] between the parties according to good reason and conscience and in reverence of God etc.

The answer of Mathew Andrewe to Henry Denys's bill.

Mathew Andrewe having made protestation that the matter contained in the bill is not sufficient in law nor in conscience to require an answer, said for declaration of truth and for answer that after the agreement between Henry Denys and himself had been concluded as stated in the bill he had arranged for the ship, *James of Ottermouth*, to be taken to London, and by his own efforts and at his own cost had purchased an adequate safe conduct from the admiral of France to protect it and its crew, and whatever cargo it took on board in the port of London, from Frenchmen during its voyage thence to Topsham in accordance with the agreement. As soon as it had reached London the master of the ship had notified Henry Denys of its arrival and that a safe conduct had been obtained by Mathew Andrewe, and had requested him to bring his merchandise to the ship to be conveyed from London to Topsham as agreed. However, Henry had not done so, but had allowed the ship to remain in London for the next 6 weeks for lack of freight and had then fully discharged Mathew from the bargain and utterly refused to load any merchandise in the ship, or to pay any freight in accordance with the bargain. Whereupon the master had agreed and covenanted with a certain William Isaak to freight the ship with such merchandise as he would bring to it to be taken to Topsham; and after the making of this agreement, Henry Denys had brought certain merchandise to the ship to be taken to Topsham, but only by arrangement between him and William Isaak, and he had not shipped madder or other merchandise by virtue of the previous agreement with Mathew Andrewe as was alleged in his answer.[3] All this Mathew Andrewe was ready to prove in whatever way the court would award, and he prayed to recover his costs and damages for his trouble and to be dismissed from the court.

The replication of Harry Denys to the answer of Mathew Andrewe.

Harry Denys, having made protestation that Mathew Andrewe's answer and the matter contained in it did not refute his bill,[4] said for his replication that at the time when he had been notified that the said ship had come to London, there had been some iron and other merchandise in it which it had conveyed to London by sea, and he had shipped madder and woad, valued at £140, in it by virtue of the bargain between himself and Mathew Andrewe, within three days after this merchandise had been unloaded, to be conveyed to Topsham in the belief that Mathew had obtained an adequate safe conduct, and because he had not got it the ship and merchandise had been carried off on the sea by Frenchmen. And Harry Denys had not caused the master and ship to remain in London for 6 weeks or any other time for lack of freight except for the reason given above, nor had he discharged Mathew Andrewe of his bargain nor refused to ship any merchandise in the ship or pay for freight as had been alleged in Mathew's answer.

Moreover Harry Denys said William Isaak, named in Mathew's answer, had approached him when he was loading the madder and woad and pressed him to allow him to ship certain merchandise of his in Harry's name to be taken to Topsham, which Harry agreed to, and in consequence Isaak had shipped some madder and woad with Harry's. Harry said also that his own madder and woad in the ship had been of the value of £140 without that shipped in his name by William Isaak.

And since Mathew Andrewe had not denied that he had agreed with Harry Denys to obtain a safe conduct from the king of France or his admiral to safeguard the ship, its merchants, crew and all its contents from the danger of seizure by Frenchmen on the sea for the whole time of its journey from the port of London to the town of Topsham, nor that the ship and merchandise had been taken by the French, Harry Denys prayed that Mathew Andrewe be ruled to satisfy him of the value of his madder and woad. Harry was ready to prove all these matters as the court should award as far as reason and conscience required.

[1] Opisham
[2] *dewe right wysnes maybe mynystred*
[3] ' answer ' is presumably in error for ' bill.'
[4] *is not sufficient to the bill*

89b

C1/51/152 *Latin*

Mandate from Edward, king of England and France etc., to Roger Keys and William Spryg, clerks, authorizing them to examine John Chanon' concerning the truth of a complaint in the petition recently presented before the king in chancery by Henry Denys of London, grocer, against Mathew Andrewe, and also of the matters contained in the answer and replication made by the parties in the same case; and by very careful and considered scrutiny of all the particulars of the complaint, answer and replication to discover the justice of the matter; and, in order to do so, having viewed the petition, answer and replication which had been enclosed with the mandate, and studied their contents, to summon John Chanon to come before them at an appointed time and place, to examine him diligently upon the gospels concerning the foregoing, and to certify the tenor of the examination and send it with this writ, under their separate seals, to the king in chancery one month after Michaelmas next. Witnessed by the king at Westminster 24 June 1477. Morton.

Endorsed: By the chancellor.

89c

C1/51/151 *Latin. Some words illegible*

To Edward, king of England and France etc. His two humble subjects, Roger Keys and William Spryg, clerks, state that they had lately received royal letters of mandate to which were attached a complaint, answer and replication in the vulgar tongue; and, both of them having scrutinized the letters and enclosures and understood them, had summoned John Chanon' and had him brought before them in a chapel in Roger Keys' house within the walls of Exeter on Wednesday 13 August 1477; and, having sworn him upon the gospels, diligently examined him concerning the particulars of the matters in the foregoing complaint, answer and replication as ordered, and took the depositions in the following words:-

(*English*) John Chanon of Sidmouth in Devonshire, lately a seaman in Mathew Andrewe's ship, the *James of Ottermouth*, strictly charged and examined by Roger Keys' and William Spryg said and deposed that he could not testify or depose anything certain concerning the bargain, covenant and agreement made at Topsham between Harry Denys and Mathew Andrewe as set out in Henry Deny's bill of complaint because he was not present when it was made.

He had, however, also said and deposed that the ship, in which he had been a seaman at the time, had sailed from the port of Topsham on 8 September 1474 and had entered the port of London about 14 days later, and soon afterwards the master and the purser and others had informed Henry Denys, notifying him that Mathew Andrewe's ship had arrived with a safe conduct purchased by Mathew from the admiral of France, and requiring him to bring his merchandise to the ship to be taken from London to Topsham, but he had not done so, causing the master, seamen and ship to remain in London for lack of freight for 14 days and more, by which delay he had discharged Mathew of their bargain and agreement, and he had also utterly refused to ship any merchandise in the ship or to pay any freight. Whereupon the master—considering Mathew Andrewe to be wholly discharged of the bargain by Henry Denys, who had caused the ship to be completely without freight—had agreed, bargained and covenanted with one, William Isaak, that he should freight the ship with such merchandise as he would bring to it to be conveyed to Topsham. After which Henry Denys had made a bargain with William Isaak by virtue of which alone he had brought certain merchandise to the ship to be conveyed to Topsham in William Isaak's name and, had not shipped any madder, woad or anything else by virtue of any bargain made between himself and Mathew Andrewe as he was alleging.

Latin

Which examination taken as above stated by Roger Keys and William Spryg, sealed by the seals of both of them, together with the writ and matters attached to it was sent into chancery as ordered for consideration.

89d

C1/54/88

CHANCELLOR The bishop of Lincoln

DATE 25 February 1475–3 September 1480

PETITIONER Mathew Andrewe

COMPLAINT Henry Denys of London, grocer, had come to Topsham[1] in Devonshire on 4[2] August 1474 and there and then by his bare word before adequate witnesses[3] had contracted with the petitioner that the latter should equip a ship, the *James*, then in his possession, with all its gear and with a safe conduct obtained from the admiral of France and send it to the port of London, and Henry Denys would then load it with such merchandise as he wished within five days after its arrival, to be taken back to Topsham, paying £10 for the journey to and from London and the freight. The petitioner had duly equipped the ship and provided the admiral of France's safe conduct and had it brought to the port of London with a master, purser and other seamen in accordance with the contract. On its arrival there the purser and seamen had notified Henry Denys that it had come and requested that he should load it with such merchandise as he pleased so that they might sail during the five days following. Nevertheless he had allowed the ship to remain unfreighted for 8 days and more, and then he had said that he would not freight it nor put any merchandise in it. As a result the master and purser with all their seamen were delayed there for 15 days, to the petitioner's great cost, before they were able to depart.

On their homeward journey the ship, men and 4 tuns of the petitioner's wine and other merchandise of his and other's had been taken by Frenchmen because the safe conduct had expired owing to the long delay in London. In consequence he had had to pay £40 for ransom of the men, and had lost his ship, valued at 100 marks, whereas had Henry Denys kept to the contract made between them the safe conduct would have lasted long enough to have protected the ship and crew from the French. Therefore the petitioner would be utterly undone by the breaking of the contract without the chancellor's goodwill on this behalf, since he had no remedy at common law.

REQUEST That the chancellor would carefully consider the foregoing and grant a writ *subpoena* directed to Henry Denys commanding him to appear before the king in chancery under a penalty and on a day given by the chancellor to answer the foregoing and to abide whatever the court thought to be reasonable, for the love of God etc.

Pledges of prosecution: John Elys and Robert Saperton, gentlemen of London.

Latin

Endorsed: Before the king in chancery on the morrow of St. Martin next.

[1]Opsam
[2]1 August in 89a.
[3]by nude parall' afore sufficient record.

Editor's Note. Henry Denys's petition, 89a, the answer to it and the replication were written on one parchment which was, no doubt, the document attached to the mandate sent to Roger Keys and William Spryg. There is no clear evidence to show whether it preceded Mathew Andrewe's complaint, but it seems likely that Henry Denys, having some reason to suppose that Mathew intended to make a claim against him, presented his bill in the hope of forestalling him. The only point at issue was the question as to which of them was responsible for the lack of protection by safe conduct from the French—Mathew by failing to carry out his undertaking to procure an adequate document or Henry by breaking the contract to freight the ship within a given time and causing delay in its sailing. The testimony called for by the court supported Mathew on this point and he could well have been dismissed from the case and have presented his own petition, 89d., to obtain compensation against Henry Denys.

A few years later, however, letters of safe conduct obtained by him—referred to as the king's servant—from the admiral of England for a Breton ship failed to protect it from capture by a man of Topsham and other ' pirates ' in ships of that port, to which it had been sailing with a cargo intended for the ransom of Bretons who had been taken prisoner in England during an outbreak of hostilities with Brittany (*CPR 1476–85* p. 520). He had given an undertaking to two Spanish merchants, living in London, to deliver a specified number of bales of wool on two given dates at Topsham or Exeter, and if he failed to do so, to appear before the king and council and abide by their decision in the matter. This was dated 31 March; he was commissioned apparently a few days later, with others, to inquire into the seizure by Englishmen off the coast of Brittany of a Breton ship loaded with bales of ' woad ' by the same Spanish merchants (*CCR 1476–85* p, 361; *CPR 1476–85* p. 426). He seems to have been employed as a customs officer and to have incurred debts to the crown (Ibid. p. 262, 328).

90a

Ci/67/65

CHANCELLOR The bishop of Lincoln

DATE 25 February 1475–Michaelmas 1477

PETITIONERS Henry, lord Grey of Codnor,[1] Richard Tettelawe, Richard Mosse, John Haghtfeld, Walter Latham, William Thomas, and John Barton, merchants.

COMPLAINT On the Monday before the feast of St. Matthew the apostle, 1353 it was enacted by parliament that if any merchant or other person, native or foreigner, were robbed of his goods at sea and the goods came to any part of England, then the owner of them would be allowed to sue for their recovery in chancery on making due proof that they were his own, and to recover them without any suit at common law, as appeared more plainly in the statute.[2] The petitioners had been in possession of 30 packs of woollen cloth, valued at £400, in a ship called the *Marie Landregare* on the sea coast of Brittany, and had remained in possession of them until the ship with all the merchandise was plundered and taken from them on the sea by wrongdoers in a ship called the *Christopher of Exmouth*, in which Richard Duke, yeoman, Robert Smyth and Robert Russell all of Exeter in Devonshire and victuallers of the *Christopher*, had been at the time. The *Marie Landregare* and her merchandise had come to England at Exmouth, and Richard Duke, Robert Smyth and Robert Russell had taken possession of the goods by trickery,[3] knowing that they had been stolen and that they were the property of the petitioners, as would be shown more plainly by evidence which was ready to be produced before the chancellor.[4]

The petitioners had often demanded delivery of the goods from Robert Russell, still living, and from Richard Duke and Robert Smyth in their life-time and, after their deaths, from Mathew Jubbe and Joan, his wife, widow and executrice of Richard Duke, and from Elizabeth, widow and executrix of Robert Smyth, who had come into possession of the goods knowing them to be stolen, and they had refused to deliver them contrary to to right and good conscience, and still refused to do so, to the great damage of the petitioners.

REQUEST That the chancellor would consider the foregoing carefully and grant writs of *subpoena* directed to Robert Russell, Mathew, Joan and Elizabeth commanding them, and each one of them to appear before the king in chancery on a day to be fixed by the chancellor under a penalty of £200 to answer to the foregoing according to the statute, and to do and receive what faith and conscience would require: for the love of God etc.

Pledges of prosecution: Thomas Maron; draper, William Tarrowe, tailor, both of London.

[1]Cottenoure
[2]27 Edw. III st. 2, cap. 13. The chancery court was not mentioned.
[3]*by subtill meanes*
[4]*as affore your lordship by evident mater redy to be shewed more pleynely shall appere*

90b

C1/67/62

The answer of Mathew Jubbe and Joan, his wife, widow of Richard Duke, to the bill of Harry, lord Grey of Codnor and the others named in the bill.

They said that the bill was not sufficient nor certain in law and conscience to require an answer—nevertheless for simple declaration of truth and by protestation, not admitting that Richard Duke had ever been a victualler of the ship, the *Christopher*, or had been in her as alleged—they said for answer that they knew nothing, except through the petitioners' complaint, of the taking of the ship, the *Mary Landregare* and the merchandise and goods in her, or of their coming into the hands of Richard Duke. They

denied that Joan was Richard Duke's executrix or had administered any
of his goods; and that any goods and merchandise from the *Mary Landregare* had come into their possession. They were ready to prove the truth
of all this in any way thought reasonable; and prayed to be dismissed with
their reasonable costs and expenses.

90c

C1/67/63

The answer of Robert Russell to the bill of Henry, lord Grey, Richard
Tettelawe and the others named in the said bill.

Robert said that the bill was insufficient in law and conscience to
require an answer; but for plainer declaration he said that he and several
others had victualled the ship, the *Christopher*, and she had been lying,
thus victualled, in Dartmouth harbour at the time when Richard, late
earl of Warwick, had fled from England into France; and the earl, with a
large number of people, had taken the *Christopher*, against Robert Russell's
will, and many other ships to cross the sea. Robert did not know what had
been done with the ship after that and had never victualled her at any
other time. He denied any knowledge of the taking of the ship, the *Mary*,
and the merchandise and goods in her by the *Christopher*, and that he had
heard, except by the petitioners' complaint, that the *Mary* and her
merchandise and goods had been taken as alleged in the bill. He also
denied that he had been in the *Christopher*, and that the merchandise and
goods or any part of them had come into his hands as alleged. All of
which he is ready to prove as the court would award, and he prayed to be
dismissed from the court with reasonable costs and damages for the
vexation and trouble he had sustained.

90d

C1/67/64

The answer of Elizabeth, widow of Robert Smyth, to the bill of Henry, lord
Grey, Richard Tettelawe and the others named in the bill.

Elizabeth said that the bill was insufficient in law and conscience to
answer, but for plainer declaration, and by protestation, not admitting
that her husband, Robert Smyth, had been a victualler of the ship, the
Christopher, said for answer that he had not been in the ship, and that none
of the merchandise and goods had come into his possession as alleged in the
bill. She also said that none of the merchandise and goods had come into
her possession and that she never knew that the ship, the *Mary*, nor any
of the merchandise and goods in her, had been taken as alleged in the
bill. All of which she was ready to prove in whatever way the court
awarded, and she prayed to be dismissed with reasonable costs and damages
for the vexation and trouble she had sustained.

90e

C1/67/65 *Endorsement Latin*

Memorandum that, during Michaelmas term in 1477, a day had been given to the parties by their consent to produce witnesses to prove the matter contained in the bill on the 3 February next. And that during Hilary term, in the same year, day had been given to the parties peremptorily during the third week in the Easter term, at which time a further day was given peremptorily by consent of the parties and in the presence of the council, on the quindene of Trinity term, before the king in chancery.

On which day, a further memorandum was made that, on 28 June 1478, the petition of Henry Grey, lord of Codnor, Richard Tettelawe, Richard Mosse, John Haghtfeld, Walter Latham, William Thomas and John Barton, merchants, against Robert Russell of Exeter and Elizabeth, widow of Robert Smyth, was presented before the king in chancery. And the answers and examinations of witnesses, depositions and other proofs having been made in due form in chancery, and having been seen, read, and heard, and fully understood, it was considered and adjudged, after careful deliberation by Thomas, bishop of Lincoln, chancellor, and by authority of the chancery court that, because the petitioners had not sufficiently proved the truth of their cause, Robert Russell and Elizabeth, and each of them, were exonerated from the allegations in the petition and absolved from the petitioners' claim, and they were dismissed *sine die* by the chancellor and by authority of the court, wholly and finally acquitted.

Editor's Note. Richard, earl of Warwick, fled from England with West-country ships to France in 1470. After his return the following year, he was killed at the battle of Barnet in 1471 (Jacob, 1969, pp. 558, 568).

Henry Grey, recently of London, knight, otherwise of Codnor in Derbyshire or Lord Grey, was pardoned for all his offences and for all debts, accounts and arrears due to the king on 30 May 1480. He was frequently on commissions of the peace and of array and for other purposes in the midlands between 1469 and 1484, and in May of the latter year Richard III granted him various manors and lordships for his good service against the rebels. (*CPR 1476–85* pp. 198, 433 and *passim*. See also Ibid. *1467–77 passim*).

91

C1/54/150

CHANCELLOR The bishop of Lincoln

DATE 28 September 1475–3 September 1480

PETITIONER John Robert of Tregony, mercer

COMPLAINT Thomas Tresithuy, county Cornwall, gentleman, and William Treuennor, gentleman, each recently granted to the king £9 2s. 6d. of lawful money towards his expedition overseas, to be paid to him or his assignees on the previous 12 May as appeared more plainly in the bills made and sealed by each of them, which the petitioner had ready to show. Since the petitioner was a merchant who came to London in the way of business, Thomas Tresithuy and William Treuennor had specially requested him to pay the said sums when he was in London and to take the bills with him. They had promised faithfully to reimburse him on his return home and he, trusting their promise, had paid the sums and had the bills in his possession and had often shewed them and requested repayment, but they were utterly refusing contrary to right and conscience. The petitioner had no remedy in the common law courts without the chancellor's goodwill on this behalf.

REQUEST That he would consider the foregoing and grant writs *subpoena* directed to Thomas Tresithuy and William Treuennor commanding them to appear before the king and council on a day given and under a penalty fixed by the chancellor to answer concerning the foregoing and to abide what right and conscience required, at the reverence of God etc.

Pledges of prosecution: John Tranowe, gentleman, William Brayton, yeoman, both of London.
Endorsed: A month from Easter next. Before the king and his council.

Editor's Note. Edward IV went to France with an army in the summer of 1475. The bishop of Lincoln became chancellor for the second time at the end of September in that year.

92

C1/67/294

CHANCELLOR The bishop of Lincoln

DATE June 1480–29 July 1485

PETITIONER Thomas Perche, merchant of Dartmouth.

COMPLAINT The petitioner had been bound to John Ley by an obligation, dated 4 May 1478, for £9 for freighting part of the ship, *Marie Bowier*, of Dartmouth, to go to Flanders. The sum was to be paid to him in Flemish money within twenty days of the ship's arrival at Welyng in Zeeland; and after it had arrived there John Ley had accepted goods of the petitioner's worth the sum of £9 in accordance with the agreement previously made between them, as the petitioner, who had been in Brabant at the time, would prove before the chancellor by several English merchants. Two years later John Ley was in Dartmouth and the petitioner had sought the return of his obligation. John Ley had sworn and testified before honest men there that he had cancelled and destroyed[1] it and because the petitioner trusted him and had previously had many dealings with him he did not ask him for an acquittance. Now John Ley, notwithstanding the receipt of the goods and his oaths and out of his dishonest disposition, had sued a plaint of debt of £9 against the petitioner before the bailiffs in Bristol, and since the latter had no acquittance to show, John Ley would recover the £9 to the petitioner's great damage, and contrary to reason and conscience, without the chancellor's goodwill on this behalf.

REQUEST That the chancellor would consider the foregoing and grant a writ of *certiorari* to the bailiffs of Bristol to bring the action before the king in chancery on a given day to be judged there according to conscience, and also a writ *subpoena* to John Ley commanding him to appear in chancery on a given day to be compelled to produce the obligation there to be cancelled, as good reason and conscience required, for the love of God etc.

Pledges of prosecution of London: William Comfort, tailor, John Wattys.

¹*broken*

93

Ci/60/165

CHANCELLOR The bishop of Lincoln

DATE 25 February 1475–79 July 1485

PETITIONERS William Gaske and Thomas Yog.

COMPLAINT The two petitioners and William Pynnewe, deceased, had been owners in possession of a ship, the *Mary of Asshe*, and because William Gaske had been charged with various sums of money owed to certain persons for the debts of William Pynnewe,¹ the latter had given all the goods and chattels of which he was possessed in England and elsewhere to William Gaske by a deed, which would be produced, and which had been acknowledged and enrolled before the mayor of London, so that William Gaske should reimburse himself against the creditors at all times. Where-upon William Gaske had immediately entered the ship and taken pos-session of William Pynnewe's third part, and a certain John Rouland of Plymouth, alleging without specialty that 50 marks was owed to him by Pynnewe, and because the petitioners were bound to various English merchants by a charter party to have the ship ready in a short time to leave England for Spain and Seville, had maliciously caused it to be arrested by reason of an action brought by him against the petitioners before the water bailiff of Sutton Pool where Rouland was both judge and party, contrary to right and good conscience. Wherefore the petitioners were likely to suffer great cost and damage by the hindrance of their voyage without the chancellor's goodwill on this behalf.

REQUEST That he would consider the foregoing carefully and grant a *certiorari* directed to the water bailiff of Sutton Pool commanding him to appear before the king in the chancery court to answer the foregoing, and that the chancellor would direct whatever he thought reasonable in accordance with reason and good conscience, for the love of God etc.

Endorsed: Before the king in his chancery on the octave of St. Michael next.

[1]*dyverse summes of money wheryn the seid William Gaske was charged to certeyr persones for the dute of the seid William Pyrnewe to dyverse his creditours*

Editor's Note. The wording of this petition is rather obscure but the inference seems to be that the water bailiff of Sutton Pool for whom the petitioners were requesting a writ *certiorari* was John Rouland against whom the complaint was made. He had been a collector of customs in Plymouth and Fowey and adjacent places sometime before 22 November 1477 on which date he received a pardon for all offences committed by him and for all debts, accounts and arrears etc., due from him to the king (*CPR 1476–85* p. 58). William Gaske and Thomas Yog, described as of Saltash and Plymouth respectively and both ' alias of London, vyntner,' with many others of Devon, Cornwall and Somerset, received general pardons in 1482 but these excepted debts etc., owed to the exchequer on account of holding office as collector of customs in any port (Ibid. p. 262).

94

C1/60/116

CHANCELLOR The archbishop of York

DATE October 1482–9 April 1483

PETITIONER Harry Hornbroke of the county of Devonshire, merchant.

COMPLAINT The petitioner and Thomas Croppe of Plymouth in the same county, merchant, had been owners of a ship, the *Andrew*, on 14 October 1482 and had freighted it from Plymouth to Nantes overseas to be loaded there with wine and other merchandise. After this had been done, they, the ship and goods had been captured on the way home by Voon Laurauns Reverquyveke and Henry Fologh of Brittany in a ship of war, the *Mary Brest*,[1] and taken into Penmarch in Brittany. The petitioner and Thomas Croppe had been landed at Brest. Afterwards they made a bargain at Plymouth in Devon that the petitioner should take over all Thomas Croppe's part of the ship and goods for the sum of 100 écus,[2] which he had paid to Thomas at Plymouth except for £7, and he had given an obligation for £10 binding himself to pay the £7 within the following five years. But Thomas Croppe had later gone to Brittany, where the ship and goods had been taken, and had affirmed that they were his, and had forged a letter of attorney, purporting to have been made in his favour by the petitioner through which the petitioner had been involved in legal expenses there of £20 and more, and he was barred from obtaining recovery of the ship and goods in accordance with the bargain by Thomas's claim to them.[3] After which the petitioner had demanded of Thomas at Plymouth in the county of Devon that he should repay the money previously paid to him, or else make an adequate testimonial addressed to the judges in Brittany, where the ship and goods were, proving that they belonged to the petitioner. But Thomas was refusing to do either, contrary to reason and conscience, and the petitioner had no remedy at common law and was likely to be undone without the chancellor's goodwill on this behalf.

REQUEST That he would consider the foregoing carefully and grant a writ *subpoena* directed to Thomas Croppe commanding him to appear before the king in chancery under a penalty and on a day fixed by the chancellor to do whatever right and conscience required on this behalf, for the love of God etc.

Pledges of prosecution: John Kyrton and Thomas Broke, both of London, gentlemen.
    Endorsed: Before the king in his chancery three weeks after Easter next.

[1]*Brast*
[2]A French silver crown piece.
[3]The language of the original is very obscure but this seems to be the gist of the petitioner's complaint against Croppe.

95

C1/76/105

CHANCELLOR The bishop of Worcester

DATE 22 August 1485–6 March 1486

PETITIONER Richard Challerton, citizen of the city of London

COMPLAINT The petitioner had covenanted in Dartmouth in the county of Devon with Thomas Gale, who was under-admiral there at the time, for a safe conduct of 60 tons for one, Jac a John, of Guerande in Brittany but Thomas Gale had made the safe conduct for 30 tons only so that the petitioner, seeing this deception, had refused it; whereupon Thomas Gale had requested him to have it and send it to Jac a John and, if it were used,[1] then Thomas Gale would be paid for it, and if not he would take it back without any payment. The safe conduct was therefore sent to Jac a John who refused it because it was not adequate or lawful and returned it to the petitioner, who took it to Thomas Gale and showed it and his undertaking about it[2] to him, and he took it back and they parted. But lately Thomas Gale had demanded payment for the safe conduct from the petitioner in the town of Exeter, and had arrested him and caused him to be put to great trouble and cost, maliciously intending great damage and hindrance to him. He also intended to empanel an inquest against the petitioner in Exeter and to condemn him in a certain sum of money, contrary to right and conscience and although the constitutions and ordinances of the town of Exeter provided that no suit was allowed there unless a trespass had been committed in the town or within its franchise. Moreover the sergeant of the town had, so the petitioner had been credibly informed, promised Thomas Gale that no jury would find against him in this matter.[3]

REQUEST That the chancellor would consider the foregoing carefully and graciously grant a *certiorari* to be directed to the mayor, receiver and steward of Exeter commanding them strictly to certify the action, pending before them, in the king's high court of chancery by a day and under a penalty fixed by the chancellor, and that he would rule what he thought was most in accordance with right and conscience; for the love of God etc., and the petitioner would pray daily to God for the chancellor.

Endorsed: Before the king in chancery one month after Michaelmas.

[1]*if ever it were occupied*
[2]*how it was allowed*
[3]*no quest passe ayenst hym for the same*

Editor's Note. The chancellor addressed in this petition was the first to serve under Henry VII. Although not referred to as deputy or under admiral, Thomas Gale had been constantly employed by the crown during the reigns of Edward IV and Richard III. He was collector of customs and subsidy in the port of Exeter and Dartmouth and adjacent places in 1477, and in December of that year he was described as ' the king's servant ' in a commission, issued on his complaint, concerning the capture of a ship when—he alleged—his attorneys had been put ashore, naked, in Ireland. He had been granted a licence in February 1477 exempting him from the provisions of the statute 20 Henry VI (1441–2) cap. v., which forbade customs officers to own ships or carry on trade, or hold wharves, quays, inns or taverns, or act as agents for foreign merchants. Still a customs officer in Exeter and Dartmouth in 1482 he, like many others, received a general pardon, which however did not cover offences against the crown committed in the course of his official duties. He was on a commission appointed in connection with the departure from court of a defendant in a case of plunder in 1483. He was one of four men commissioned in October 1484 to deal with a complaint brought by Richard Challerton, who, two and a half years earlier, had left his kinsman in Bordeaux as a pledge for the fulfilment of a promise to send some woollen cloth from England in part payment for wine acquired in Bordeaux. The wine was shipped in a Breton vessel, no English one being available, and the cloth was duly loaded in the same ship, but both it and the cloth were captured on the return voyage by a ship of Fowey, and the kinsman was held a prisoner for lack of the cloth, and also for ransom due to hostilities with France. To redeem him, Richard Challerton loaded another Breton ship in Dartmouth. This was also taken by another ship of Fowey, and he brought an action for restitution against the master and owner. (*CPR 1476–85* pp. 13, 79. 249, 345, 517.)

Thomas Gale was also granted the office of keeper or clerk of the king's ships for life, and was commissioned to take the muster of the force going to sea to resist the enemy—both in 1485, shortly before the death of Richard III at Bosworth Field (Ibid. pp. 533, 545).

96

C1/78/145

CHANCELLOR John, bishop of Worcester

DATE 22 August 1485—6 March 1486

PETITIONERS Roger Werth and Walter Yorke, citizens of the city of Exeter.

COMPLAINT The petitioners had recently loaded a boat of Polruan (John Cornelys, master) in the water of Fowey with 61 pieces of Cornish tin; and it had been lying there, still loaded, for six weeks or more in great uncertainty and danger,[1] all because of the chicanery[2] of John Menheneke, mayor of the town of Lostwithiel, and Luke[3] Fryse. The latter had brought a plaint before the same mayor and burgesses of that town, and they had arrested the boat and tin and were still holding them under arrest, not allowing the petitioners to have delivery of their own goods by finding sufficient security to the court, nor continuing the proceedings against them according to the law, but seeking, unfairly and unlawfully by all the devices that they could, to delay the boat and tin until it was perished and overturned by bad weather, to the utter undoing of the petitioners, contrary to all good law, reason and conscience without the chancellor's goodwill in this behalf.

REQUEST That he would consider the foregoing carefully and grant a certiorari directed to the mayor and burgesses of Lostwithiel commanding them to send the cause of the arrest of the boat with all the circumstances concerning it before the king in chancery on a certain day, and to carry out there whatever the court awarded in this behalf, and the petitioners would pray to God for the long life of the chancellor.

[1] in grete doute and perele
[2] subtile meanes
[3] Luce

97

C1/96/41

CHANCELLOR John, archbishop of Canterbury

DATE 6 October 1486—6 October 1493

PETITIONER Elizabeth Hourde, widow, executrix of the will of William Hourde.

COMPLAINT Fifteen years earlier, John Leche of Fowey had taken upon himself to rescue goods and chattels valued at 100 marks belonging to William Hourde, out of a ship, the Barbara of Fowey, which had been wrecked in Fowey harbour, and had them in his possession; and he had promised to bind himself to William Hourde to satisfy him for whatever was their true value.

William Hourde having died, the petitioner, as excutrix of his will, had requested John Leche over and over again[1] to deliver the goods and chattels, which he had absolutely refused to do contrary to all right and good conscience. Since the petitioner did not know in detail of what the goods and chattels consisted, and had no specialty which she could produce, she was without remedy at the common law of the land unless the chancellor bestowed on her his special aid in this behalf.

REQUEST That he would consider the foregoing carefully and grant a writ *subpoena* directed to John Leche commanding him to appear before the king in chancery on a certain day and under a certain penalty fixed by the chancellor, and, then and there, be directed as the chancellor thought most in accordance with right and good conscience in this behalf, at the reverence of God etc.

Pledges of prosecution: Thomas Broun, yeoman, Robert John, tailor, both of London.

Endorsed: Before the king in his chancery on the octave of Trinity next.

[1]*oftymes and many*

Editor's Note. The wreck of the *Barbara of Fowey* probably took place some time after 1472. A vessel of that name, of which William Hourde was part owner, had been successfully employed free-booting at about that time. The ship's master and William Hourde himself, eleven named men (including ' Broun, goldsmith', cp. 64 and 71 above) and others were sued in the chancery by merchants of Brittany for capturing and disposing of some 14 ships and their cargoes, contrary to the treaty between Edward IV and the duke of Brittany, on various dates in the spring of 1469. The names or descriptions of the ships and the value of the goods and merchandise taken from each of them, with the names of the owners, were set out in the commission of inquiry which was issued in the following July. Three years later, in April 1472, three merchants of Bristol and the master of one of two ships of Spain complained of the capture of the ships and their cargoes of woollen cloths and wine by the *Edward* and the *Barbara* (*CPR 1467–77* pp. 197, 354, 378).

William Hourde, esquire, had been granted 10 marks annually for life from the issues of the duchy of Cornwall in 1468, to date from 1466 (Ibid. p. 83, *CCR 1468–76* p. 4).

INDEX

Roman numerals (in lower case) refer to pages of the Introduction; arabic numerals to the numbers of the items in the text; and 'note' to the Editor's Note in the text; textual footnotes are prefixed by n.
Names of persons are given in the spelling used in the text, followed in brackets by variants. Place-names are given whenever possible in the modern form used in the text, followed within brackets in italics by the form or forms found in original documents.

ABBOT, JOHN AND ROBERT, 27
Abervynges (Brittany), 26
Abingdon (Berks.), 66
Account, action of, 86
Acquittance, forged, 6; made under duress, 23, 49
Adam, John and Peter, of London, 68 note; Thomas, of Polruan, shipmaster, 33, 65 and note, 74 note
Admiral of England, xi, xii, 13; see Beaufort, Thomas; Exeter, duke of; Kent, earl of; Rutland, earl of; of France, 89; deputy of, xi, 18 note, 22, 26, 28; lieutenant of, 6; underadmiral, 95
Admiralty, court of, xi–xii, xiv, 3 note, 13, 55; in Devonshire, 13; at Horton Key, 87; marshal of, 23; vice-marshal, xii, 13
Adventure (trading), 17, 78
Aisshman, Thomas, 53
Alabaster images, 4
Aleyn, John of Penryn, 18
Alfonso, Fernando of Lisbon, 1
Algarve (Portugal), 19
Aliens, see Foreigners
Alum, 40
Amiens (France), 21
Ancient Petitions, x n. 2, 10 note, 11 note
Andrew, John, vice-marshal of the admiralty court, 13
Andrewe, Mathew (Matthew), of Topsham, 89
Aquitaine (France), 65
Aragon (Spain), 37 note, 71
Arbitration, 14, 45 note
Arnell, Richard, 51b
Arnold, Edmund (Esmond), of Dartmouth, 2, 13
Arrest, of men, 10b, 24, 44, 47, 86; of boat, 96; of goods, 17, 26, 31; of ship in king's service, 8: of ships, 6, 26, 44, 77
Arundell, sir John of, 18; of Trerys, 54; John of, esq, 64 note, 65 note; sheriff of Cornwall, 72e; sir Thomas, 54; William, earl of, 83 note; lady, 10b
Aspernine, Thomas, 49
Assh, John, 20
Asshton (Aisshton), Nicholas, 55ab, 67b, 68 note
Aston, Robert, of Newport, Isle of Wight, 48ab

Attachment, 68–9
Atterede (Attred), John, 65, 71c
Attorney, 48b, 65, 67; of Edward prince of Portugal, 1; king's, 75c; for merchants of Rouen, 30; letters of, forged, 94
Aunger, Henry, of St. Ives, 43
Ayton, Thomas, 61

BABBE, JOHN, 28
Bachelor, Walter, king's searcher in Dartmouth, 2
Bailiffs, xi; of Bristol, 92; Dartmouth, 11, 25 note, 46a, 47, 55d; Penryn, 18; Southampton, 4 and note, 61, 88; Topsham, 66, 74; earl of Warwick, 26; water, see water bailiff
Bailly, John, 2, 55b
Baker, Aleyn, of Dartmouth, 79; John, of Fowey, 5; Richard, of Dartmouth, 79
Bakeston, Piers, French prisoner, 61
Balard, John and Ronald, of Fowey, 5
Balyn, John, of Brittany, 68
Barbour, William, of Newport, 48
Barcelona, in Catalona, 71a
Barell, John, of Cornwall, 56
Barnstaple, 51ab, 58, 78, 82 note
Baron, John, 28 note; of Exeter, 35–6
Barowe, John Harry, 72e
Barton, John, 90ae
Bath, Bath and Wells, bishop of, see Chancellors
Bay, the, in Brittany, 73; salt of, 48a
Bayonne (Basses-Pyrénées), 72, seaman of, 37 note
Beaumond, John, of Tavistock, 53
Beauchamp, Richard, of Guernsey, 27
Beaufort, Thomas, 13 note
Beaumont (Bemond), Philip, esq, 82
Beddwyn, Richard, 64
Bekerton, Henry, 5
Bele, William, of Exminster, 40
Belle Isle (France), 19
Bench, Common, x, 11; chief justice of, 75c; King's, xiii, 71j; chief justice of, 75c
Benefeld, Simon, of Shoreham, 10b
Benett, Henry, 71i
Benteley (Benteleigh), William, 12, 20; lieutenant of the admiral, xii, 16
Berdwyk, John, admiral's deputy, 22
Bere, John, of Barnstaple, 58; Peter, of Plympton, 53; Thomas, commissioner, 55ab, 57

Chanon, John, of Sidmouth, 89bc
Charleton, John, 2
Charter party, 16 and note, 93
Chasault, Piers, of Limousin, 61
Chattoye, William, 29a, 30
Cherbourg (Normandy), captain of, 38; siege of, 18
Chiddley, James, 30
Chilterne, John, of Marborough, 52
Chinals, Sampson, of Fowey, 5
Chirche, John, of London, 33
Chudley, James, 67d
Cinque Ports, xiii; warden of, 39
Classon, Clays, of Dunkirk, shipmaster, 32 and note
Cleeve (Clyve, Clive, in Devon), David abbot of, 82; ship of, 34
Clement, John, and William, of Dartmouth, 24 and note, 79
Clemowe, William, 69
Clerk, James de, of Sluis, Flanders, 32; John of New Salisbury, 80; John, esq. 29a; Thomas, of Ireland, 57
Clerk of the rolls, 29c, 48b
Clinton, Piers, 70c
Close rolls, entries on, x
Cloth, 4, 26, 36, 62; canvas, 49, 63, 73 n.3, 76; crese, 27, 28, note, 63; Dyneham, 49; frieze, Irish, 70b, Welsh, 76; linen, 28 note, 37, 53; long, 34; small, 63; straits, 76, 78; vitry, 73; woollen, 90a, 95 note, 97 note
Clyveden (Cliveden, Clyfden), Richard, 48b, 52
Codnor, Henry, lord Grey of, 90a–e
Cok, John, of Bodmin, 84; Walter, 79
Coke, Henry, 79; William of Bodinnick, 54
Cocket, 34, 46b, 76
Colan, Thomas, of Bodinnick, 54
Colaton, John, 85
Colege, John, 54; Thomas, 49
Colman, Richard, of Marlborough, 52
Colshull, John, knight, 64 and note 68 note, 71c
Colville, John, of Plymouth, shipmaster, 1, 37 and note
Colyn, Ralf, 20
Comfort, William, of London, 92
Common bench, *see* Bench
Common law, x, xviii, 11, 13, 21, 28, 31, 49, 55a, 64, 70c, 80, 81, 85, 86, 87, 89a, 91, 94, 97
Conquet le (Brittany), 26, 53 and note
Cook, Richard, Mayor of Exeter, 28 and note
Cok', William, 36
Cop', John, of Barnstaple, 78
Copleston, John, 20, 28 note, 36
Cornelys, John, of Polruan, shipmaster, 96
Cornewe, John, 64, 71c
Cornyssh, John, of Plymouth, shipmaster, 32 note
Corpe, John, of Dartmouth, 10ab, 14c
Corpus cum causa, see writs
Coseyne, Martin, 26

Costs, 3, 10ab, 18; and expenses, 18, request for assessment of, 55d, for reasonable, 90bc, *see* Damages
Counsel, for petitioners, 46a
Court, of admiral, *see* admiralty; of duke of Brittany, 10 note; of mayors and bailiffs, xi, 4, 43, 78, 86; of provost of Eton, 68–9; Staple, 35; of water bailiff, 6, 31
Courteney, sir Hugh, 71c, 73–4; sir Philip, 67d and note, 79
Coventry (Warwickshire), 15
Craddok, Thomas, of Bridgwater, 51ab
Crayer, 44, 48b, 77
Crese, Henry, of Plymouth, 6
Croppe, Thomas, of Plymouth, 94
Curteys, John, of Lostwithiel, 3; Simon, of Falmouth, shipmaster, 48ab
Custom, of Topsham, 40
Customs, 1 note, 22, 76; collectors of, xi; in Exeter and Dartmouth, Thomas Gille, 39 note; in Plymouth and Fowey, John Rouland, 93 note; Southampton, 1 note; evasion of, 2, 36; rolls of, London, 34; searcher of, in Dartmouth, 2, Plymouth, 34, Southampton, 5 note

DAMAGES, 18, 55d, 58, 68, 69; security for, xviii; *see* costs
Damme (Flanders), 32
Dandy, Nicholas, shipmaster, 23
Danyell, Stephen, 55b
Danzig (Prussia), 44, 74 note, 82
Daromaye, Daramayo, Ochoa, of Spain, shipmaster, 76 and note
Dartmouth (Devon), 1, 2, 4, 7, 9 and note, 10ab, 11, 14ac, 15, 16, 22, 24, 25, 27, 32, 35 and note, 38 and note, 40, 45a–d and note, 46ab and note, 47, 49 and note, 53, 55a–d and note, 67 note, 77 and note, 79 and note, 80 and note, 83, 86, 92, 95 and note
Darundell, John, esq. of Cornwall, 59 and note
David, Hugh, 79
Davy, John, of Lyme, 83
Dawe, William, 81
Dawet (Brittany), 47
Debt, action of, 6, 68, 92
de la Motte, Michael, 60, 64
Denham, sir John, 67d
Denys, Henry, of London, 89a–d and note
Depe, George, of St. Malo, 88
Derneford, Stephen, the elder, 6
Detinue, false action of, 77
Devonshire, Humphrey, earl of, 82; lord of, 42
Dieppe (France), 48b
Dinan (Brittany), 49
Dinard (Brittany), 47
Disco, John, of Navarra, 9
Donnart, John, 28, 36
Donne, Thomas, 82 and note
Dordrecht (Danzig), 74 and note
Dorset, 27 note